OUR NATIONAL PARKS
Tours with Rangers

OUR NATIONAL PARKS
Tours with Rangers

By John M. Thompson
Photographs by Phil Schermeister

NATIONAL GEOGRAPHIC

WASHINGTON, D.C.

Preceding pages: Autumn frost melts on a fallen leaf in Yosemite National Park.

At Petrified Forest National Park, mineral-tinted layers of stone have been eroded in the Tepees area into cone-shaped hills.

Opposite: A dragonfly's wings catch the sunlight in Everglades National Park.

CANADA

WASHINGTON

MONTANA

NORTH DAKOTA

OREGON

IDAHO

SOUTH DAKOTA

WYOMING

NEBRASKA

NEVADA

UTAH

COLORADO

KANSAS

YOSEMITE
NATIONAL PARK

BRYCE CANYON
NATIONAL PARK

CALIFORNIA

ARIZONA

PETRIFIED FOREST
NATIONAL PARK

OKLA

NEW MEXICO

Pacific

Ocean

TEXAS

MEXICO

Site featured in this book

Tours with Rangers

ONTARIO

ISLE ROYALE NATIONAL PARK

ME.

MINNESOTA

MICHIGAN

VT

N.H.

CAPE COD NATIONAL SEASHORE

WISCONSIN

NEW YORK

MASS.

CONN.

R.I.

IOWA

PA.

NEW JERSEY

ILLINOIS

INDIANA

OHIO

MD.

DELAWARE

W. VA.

MISSOURI

KENTUCKY

VIRGINIA

NORTH CAROLINA

TENNESSEE

ARKANSAS

SOUTH CAROLINA

GEORGIA

Atlantic

Ocean

MISSISSIPPI

ALABAMA

LA.

FLORIDA

Gulf of Mexico

BAHAMAS

EVERGLADES NATIONAL PARK

0 ——— miles ——— 500

0 ——— kilometers ——— 500

C U B A

INTRODUCTION

Who better to guide us through the national parks than the people who know them best? The men and women in the green pants and wide-brimmed hats know their way around America's natural treasures. If you arrived at a national park and wondered, say, what was a good three-mile hike, suitable for children, having a great panorama, and perfect for pictures of sunset, you'd ask a ranger.

Now here's a chance to see what the rangers themselves like best about their parks and their jobs. More than 40 rangers were interviewed for this book, and not one of them said he or she was in the park service for the money. Several mentioned, almost as though amazed, that they were actually getting paid for doing something that other people took vacations to do. They were getting paid to hike, kayak, climb rocks, ride horses, and watch birds. And they could feel good about it because in the process they were doing the important work of preserving and protecting the park's "resources" (in park-speak) while making them available for people to enjoy.

That was one common theme that emerged from these interviews. All the rangers were enthusiastic about their work, about being in the great outdoors that they love. Several also mentioned that the best part of the job was educating people who would then become, as one ranger put it, future stewards for our national parks. One of the most interesting interviews was with Ranger Shelton Johnson of Yosemite National Park, whose angle on education was that, in an increasingly multicultural society, the parks must find ways to attract minorities if they want to continue enjoying the wide support they always have.

Though rangers by and large love their jobs, their jobs are not always easy. As one ranger explained, "We're a little bit of everything—the rescue folks, the medics, the firefighters, the police, the teachers, the traffic guards, you name it." But that variety has its own appeal.

When asked about their favorite places, some rangers talked about locations far off the beaten path, well away from the crowds. Others proudly described the most famous places within their park, suggesting maybe a time of day or year when those marquee places were best visited. One or two rangers took a more metaphysical approach to the question, saying, in effect, that it's not the place so much as the attitude—every place in the park is wonderful, as long as you take the time to slow down and fully appreciate it with all your senses. One ranger, in Everglades National Park, found it hard to even answer the question, though he did have a great deal to say about a park he cared for deeply and about whose future he was greatly concerned.

Along with all their answers about favorite places came stories. Stories about how they became rangers, about things they had seen and done in the parks. There was an amusing anecdote about wolves on Isle Royale, a harrowing rescue adventure on the cliffs of Yosemite, an awe-inspiring thunderstorm over Petrified Forest, a tree filled with roseate spoonbills in Everglades. A ranger at Zion told me about his habit of taking early morning runs and how one morning he had encountered a young woman who had gone outside to relieve herself. She was wearing no clothes and had not wanted to bother dressing and walking to the campground restroom; they bid each other an embarrassed good morning.

The book features six national parks, representing six different ecosystems. To represent swamps we've chosen Everglades; for seashores Cape Cod; for northern woodlands Isle Royale; for canyonlands Bryce Canyon; for deserts Petrified Forest; and for mountains Yosemite. Concluding each chapter are mini-profiles of two more parks within that ecosystem. The choice of parks is somewhat arbitrary; some are well known, others less so. The rangers were chosen for their articulate thoughtfulness, and I'd like to think that they represent the true voice of the national parks. Together they have spent hundreds of years in our national park system. Some are young; some are old. Some have worked at numerous parks; others have stayed at one park for nearly 30 years. What they have in common is their ardent dedication to our national park system.

—*John M. Thompson*

The amber light of evening bathes Yosemite National Park, where awe-inspiring Half Dome rises 4,800 vertical feet above the valley floor. One of the park's beloved geological landmarks, the rock face was cleaved in two by glacial action during the last ice age. Once considered inaccessible, its summit is now visited by thousands of hikers annually.

CHAPTER I

The Many Faces of Yosemite

One of the most magnificent places in the United States, Yosemite National Park ranks among a handful of destinations—New York City, Chicago, the Grand Canyon—that top most must-see lists. Its thundering waterfalls, tremendous granite domes, high meadows, and snow-clad peaks have inspired legions of visitors since its discovery by the nonnative world in the mid-19th century. Naturalist John Muir, landscape painter Albert Bierstadt, and photographer Ansel Adams are but a few of the artists whose work has exalted Yosemite into a realm of the gods. Drawn by stories and images of Yosemite's wonders, some four million annual worshipers pour into the park. Yet with its ample boundaries it retains its ability to satisfy the "wonderlust" of the casual visitor as well as the wilderness lover's need for solitude.

Interpretive ranger Margaret Eissler, who has worked in Yosemite for 20 years, embraces the fact that people are part of the Yosemite experience. Most people, especially half-day visitors, funnel into the famous Yosemite Valley. As Eissler says, "You have to go to Yosemite Valley. That's what most people think of when they think of Yosemite. They think of the photographs they've seen, or the paintings—of Half Dome, the waterfalls, the sheer rock walls. Yosemite Valley is the core of the park."

She can tick off a number of wonderful hikes from the valley to spectacular views, hikes that are well worth the effort even in the busy summer months. A hike up to Yosemite Falls, for example, yields close-ups of the highest unbroken waterfall in the continent, as well as a view of the valley from 2,425 feet above the valley floor. You can also see the iconic Half Dome, an 8,842-foot granite dome sheared by Ice Age glaciers. On the south, shady side of the valley, a rigorous walk up to Vernal and Nevada Falls offers a different angle on the valley. The waterfalls are at their pounding, misty peak of intensity in spring and early summer. "You get drenched by snowmelt up there," Eissler says, "It's like taking a cold shower."

Below snow and early morning mist, spring runoff floods a creek in Yosemite Valley. Yosemite's many faces vary not only by location but by season, each one casting its own mountain spell.

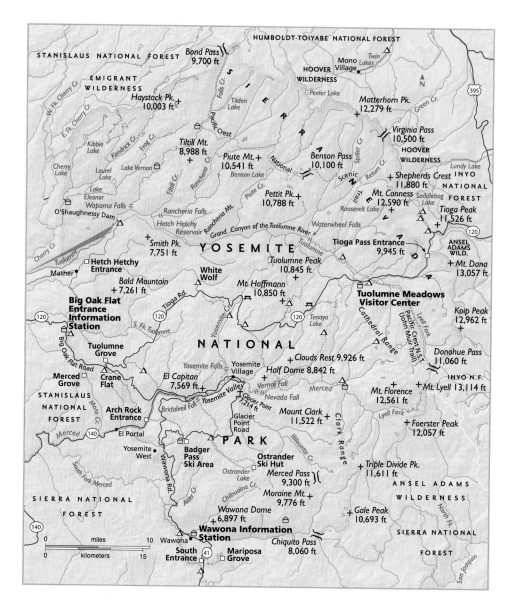

But then beyond the valley experience lies another Yosemite. Several Yosemites, in fact. And this is where things become interesting. With 90 percent of the visitors packed into the valley, the remainder of the park lies wide open. "The farther out you go the quieter it gets," maintains Eissler. And the variety of landscapes can boggle the mind. While the valley lies at 4,000 feet, Tuolumne Meadows, on the eastern end of the park, lies up at around 8,000 feet. And Tuolumne is Eissler's "center of the universe." Here is where she spent her summers as a child and where she now summers as a ranger. Her happiest memories were formed in this "most glorious playground." Who would not envy her growing up in this subalpine meadow of wildflowers and grasses, ribboned by the blue Tuolumne River and backdropped by domed rocks and horned peaks?

"I've met so many people," says Eissler, "who've forever camped in the valley, but then one day took an excursion to the higher elevations and were just amazed at what they discovered." The Tioga Road to the east side of the park, Eissler explains, gradually ascends a tilted escarpment up to the crest of the Sierra. Then from 9,945-foot Tioga Pass, on the edge of the park, the road plunges down the east side of the mountains, which is protected by national forest land.

One of the great things about Tuolumne, says Eissler, is the sense of community. "So many people have been touched by this place, and they come back summer after summer. For many, a year isn't complete without a visit. Friendships develop—friendships welded together forever with the best of memories in a most beautiful place. And there is also a larger sense of community with everything else, whether it's the river or the bears or the rocks or the domes. That's what really strikes me every year."

On the other side of the park, but also outside Yosemite Valley, lies the favorite getaway for ranger Tom Medema, branch chief for interpretive field operations. Speaking of it, he also reveals his favorite Yosemite season. "Badger Pass Ski Area is one of the oldest ski areas in the West, if not *the* oldest. It's just a great family place with a few lifts and a small day lodge, and I spend every spare moment there with my family. It's one of those places that while you wouldn't consider it a hidden gem in terms of Sierra skiing, it's a wonderfully historic area that tells the tradition of skiing in North America." And since locals tend to flock to Tahoe and other large areas, Badger Pass is never crowded. "We might stand in line behind four or five people once in a while on a holiday weekend." To Medema, who grew up in Michigan skating on a backyard ice rink, Yosemite's winter offers a chance to continue doing with his children what he loved to do growing up.

Just to the east of Badger Pass lies another historic winter center called Ostrander Ski Hut. It was built by the Civilian Conservation Corps, says Medema, at Ostrander Lake, about a ten-mile backcountry ski in from Badger Pass. People overnight there for a modest fee and then use it as a base for exploring.

One of Medema's fondest memories of Yosemite is a cross-country ski outing he took one day on Glacier Point Road, most of which is unplowed in winter. He skied all the way out to Glacier Point and had the whole place to himself. Glacier Point is one of the most spectacular viewpoints in the entire park in any season, its panorama from about 3,000 dizzying feet above Yosemite Valley sweeping almost every major landmark—Yosemite Falls, North Dome, Half Dome, the Merced River, Nevada Fall, Vernal Fall. But in winter the sensory experience is heightened tenfold. First, there is the exhilaration of skiing there. Then there is the utter silence and clarity. With a fresh blanket of snow the mountains and domes stand out in sharply etched relief.

Tom recalls the terrifying attraction of being able to ski right to the edge and feeling dwarfed by the expanse in front of him. "That experience jumps out because it was so singular, and very few people get to see Yosemite that way."

Medema also is fascinated with the unusual phenomena that winter brings. One is the almost-frozen waterfalls. Yosemite Falls dries up in early autumn, then with snowfall begins running again. It has so much spray that it freezes onto the granite walls around and behind the waterfall. "And you get these massive sheets of ice that form each day. Then when the sun comes out, they start to melt and fall. They come crashing down, and you can hear these booming crashes from sheets of ice the size of football fields that come peeling down to the valley floor." Another phenomenon is frazzle ice, when the creeks at the base of the falls turn into slush. "While we get freezing temperatures at night we often thaw during the day, and there are various states of freezing and unfreezing each day that create these unique and compelling scenes."

So what does Medema think of the high season at Yosemite? "There are a handful or two of days a year that are as bad as you've heard, and the rest of the year it's not. Certainly weekends in the summer can be quite busy, and when people don't take advantage of the shuttle we end up with some traffic gridlock. It's a controversial issue—how do we manage four million people a year, the majority coming between May and October? It's a very narrow valley, and when you shove that many people into this narrow a space you run out of room."

A typical summer day can bring more than 15,000 people to the valley. Thousands spill beyond the hotels, eateries, and souvenir shops onto the nearby trails. Even the grueling 17-mile round-trip hike up 8,842-foot-high Half Dome can attract hundreds of people a day. According to Medema there are two schools of thought on crowd control. One is to increase the urban infrastructure with more roads, parking lots, and so on; the other is to decrease urbanization by requiring use of mass transportation, bicycles, or walking. Right now the shuttle is optional, and even it is sometimes stuck in traffic. There are some late afternoons—when people are leaving the park—that Yosemite Village traffic can slow to one hour over a two-mile stretch.

Yet no matter which school of thought the park favors, backlash is sure to follow. Medema cites a recent plan to re-route traffic around Yosemite Lodge so that it does not intersect the steady stream of pedestrians on the trail to Yosemite Falls—the marquee feature in the valley. Though the current situation is untenable, redesigning the road means moving it closer to the river; the impact to the riverine environment has many people concerned. "It's a delicate balancing act of trying to

The art of basketry remains in good hands at the Native American Cultural Center in Yosemite Valley.
Hunter-gatherers arrived in the area around 1400 B.C.; the last tribe to call the valley home was a band
of Miwok who named it Ahwahnee, "the Place of the Big Mouth," for its shape.

TOURS WITH RANGERS

Wildflowers carpet misty Cook's Meadow in Yosemite Valley (opposite), while at meadow's edge a mule deer grazes (above), keeping a wary eye out for its main predator, the mountain lion. Yosemite's mule deer winter in the relatively warm Upper Sonoran Zone; in summer they move up into the Transition and Canadian Zones, the latter situated at about 7,500 feet elevation.

Water on stone: Powerful forces of nature continue to shape Yosemite National Park. Here hikers pause along the Mist Trail to watch the Merced River pounding down Vernal Fall; farther up lies another giant step in the canyon—Nevada Fall.

Following pages: Dawn paints a luminist landscape in Yosemite Valley, with the signature El Capitan rising 3,593 sheer feet on the left and Bridalveil Fall dropping 620 feet on the right. Water, ice, and time sculpted the exposed granite into the U-shaped valley visible today.

figure out what's right and what's not," says Medema. "Everything's under a microscope. Fortunately, everyone loves the park; they just have different ideas about what's best for it. For example, the Sierra Club is very engaged with what happens here, and it was critical to the development of Yosemite." Indeed the histories of Yosemite National Park and the Sierra Club are intimately intertwined. The park was officially established in 1890; two years later the conservationists who had worked to protect the area formed the Sierra Club. Its first president was "father of Yosemite National Park" John Muir.

With up to 70 percent of its visitors from in state, Yosemite is a very regionally based park, with generations of Californians feeling a strong connection to the place.

Hence Yosemite is more in the political spotlight than many other national parks. "It's an area that's steeped in controversy going all the way back to the establishment of the park, and the development of the Hetch Hetchy Reservoir," says Medema. John Muir called the Hetch Hetchy Valley "one of Nature's rarest and most precious mountain temples," but he lost a battle with the federal government to keep the Tuolumne River undammed there. "It was a seminal moment in environmental legislative history," says Medema, "and that battle is still raging today. There is a very prominent drive to restore Hetch Hetchy 90 years later that has a real head of steam." Many consider the Hetch Hetchy, in the little-visited northwest part of the park, a spectacular mini-version of Yosemite Valley and would welcome the removal of the dam. The California Department of Water Resources is reviewing the issue.

One of the most attention-grabbing spectacles at Yosemite is the sport of rock climbing. The tall sheer granite walls of Yosemite have long made it a mecca for climbers from around the world. Climbing in Yosemite has become so popular that the park has its own climbing ranger. Articulate, engaging, 28-year-old ranger Lincoln Else learned to climb in Yosemite when he was 12. While majoring in philosophy at Yale he worked summers here and continues on a seasonal basis. In the off-season he likes to go "as far as I can get from Yosemite." He has traveled and climbed in places around the world, worked for environmental groups in Washington, D.C., assisted a criminal defense attorney, and done camera work on documentaries. "Like many people who work for the park service I'm a bit schizophrenic. Half of me wants to be in the complete isolated wilderness and the other half wants to be in Times Square."

"What Yosemite is most known for are its traditional climbs," says Else, "meaning crack systems and big walls—granite cliffs that often take more than a day to climb." El Capitan and Half Dome are the most famous cliffs in the park, El Capitan being the largest at about 3,500 feet from its toe all the way up to its summit. Climbers also like El Cap for its accessibility—you can drive practically to the base of the rock. Half Dome, on the other hand, stands a long trek up from the valley and across talus slopes. At any given time there might be twenty to thirty parties (usually of two people) on El Cap, whereas on Half Dome you might find two. A typical climb to the top of El Cap takes three to five days, though some parties spend more than a week. Then, within the emerging sport of speed-climbing, there are a few super athletes who have summited El Cap in under three hours.

Else's mission, like that of any ranger, is to help preserve and protect the park while making it available for people to enjoy. As the climbing ranger, then, he helps promote his sport, while at the same time making it safe and enjoyable for all. He admits that sometimes, with such a diverse group as the climbing community, that mission

A rock climber considers his options on El Capitan. Surrounded by acres of vertical rock, climbers can spend several days on routes to the top, though speed climbers, unencumbered by bulky equipment, have mastered El Cap in just a few hours.

can be contradictory. On the other hand, he says, the climbers and backpackers often see themselves "as the people who are really pushing the limits and experiencing Yosemite to the fullest degree" and are thus more likely to be good caretakers of the place. "What it boils down to is a lot of education—teaching people to climb clean or efficiently so as not to harm the place."

It's not always a matter of simply removing your hardware from the cracks. On multi-day climbs there's the problem of human waste disposal. "If 30 people are up on the wall at any given time spread out over the face, and they're all going to the bathroom that's not a good thing. The park requires, and climbers themselves encourage, a leave-no-trace principle." In practice, roped onto a narrow ledge a thousand feet off the ground, relieving oneself can be somewhat tricky. "There's a number of ways to pull it off; most people with a little creativity manage to figure something out." It often involves the use of a paper bag, followed by storage in a plastic tube or dry river bag. "Bottom line is you're leaving nothing behind," Else jokes.

Else has personally climbed hundreds of routes in Yosemite but maintains that he is not "an adrenaline junkie." "I don't like roller coasters, and to me one of the most attractive things about climbing is the challenge of making it safe." He enjoys the mental puzzle as much as the physical test. One problem, for example, involves shlepping enough gear for several nights, but not so much that you become bogged down. Climbers haul their gear up after each rope-length pitch of about 200 feet. "If you're going to be up on the wall for seven days, you're going to have a huge amount of equipment—your sleeping bags, rain gear, emergency equipment, and water. The face of the cliff is like a desert, and you can usually drink about a gallon a day. A gallon weighs about eight pounds. So the largest challenge is often the logistics of getting that equipment up with you efficiently."

Free-soloing, or climbing without protection, gets a lot of attention from non-climbers, says Else, yet is shrugged at in the climbing community. Else compares it to climbing a ladder higher than one would care to fall from. "If someone's been climbing for years and they've climbed a certain route hundreds of times, they may get to the point where they feel that solid and comfortable in that setting." He admits that just about every climber has free-soloed some—at least gone unroped briefly in a place where a fall would almost certainly mean death. On the other hand, there are very few climbing fatalities from free-soloing. Of Yosemite's 20 to 30 annual climbing accidents, one or two might be fatal, yet there have been only a couple of free-solo deaths in Yosemite's history. Virtually no one free-solos where they don't feel utterly confident, and no one, to his knowledge, has attempted to free-solo El Cap or Half Dome.

TOURS WITH RANGERS

Staghorn lichens coat trees (above), one of which makes a fine perch for a California spotted owl (opposite). Despite habitat destruction and decreasing numbers, the spotted owls continue to hang on, particularly in protected places such as Yosemite National Park.

Instead, people have begun using Yosemite as a kind of training ground, honing skills they can then take to the Himalaya, Greenland, and other remote places. Learning to climb faster and more efficiently, climbers can then travel to traditional expedition-style areas and tackle peaks much more cleanly. Of course, Yosemite itself will always be a destination for many climbers, and Else sees more and more people coming to the sport, "through the advent of climbing gyms and the popularity of extreme sports and outdoor adventure. There's a justified fascination with all things outdoors and all things intense."

As a ranger, Else wears a number of hats—medic, firefighter, policeman, teacher, traffic guard, and rescuer. "Search-and-rescue work is a big chunk of what I do, a lot of it revolving around climbing." In fact, says Tom Medema, Yosemite has one of the best search-and-rescue (SAR) teams in the world. Interestingly, most of the rock climbing rescues are not of serious climbers. The technical challenge of getting off the ground and onto vertical granite, says Else, is generally self-limiting; plus most experienced climbers know after a couple of hundred feet whether they're up to the challenge of continuing. More common is for a casual hiker to stray onto a cliff, then find himself scrambling from cliff to cliff with no ability to get down. Yells for help are all that's needed to initiate a rescue.

Wilderness specialist Mark Fincher, who has been at Yosemite since 1988, used to coordinate many of the park's annual load of about 200 SARs. Most are a routine matter of evacuating someone with heat exhaustion, a twisted knee, or sprained ankle. But there are about a dozen high-stakes rescues off rock walls. "If we have a big early storm or a big late storm," says Fincher, "we probably will have to do multiple rescues." An October snowstorm last year stranded a number of climbers on El Cap. With conditions too risky for helicopters, the rescuers, including Lincoln Else, hiked 12 miles to the top, camped out waiting for the storm to subside, then rappelled down to climbers. Some at first waved off help, then later readily agreed to the rescue when conditions deteriorated. Others, such as two Japanese climbers on a formation called the Nose, never requested help. Though their progress was monitored by telescope from the valley, they died of exposure.

Along with the climbing rescues, Yosemite sees up to a half dozen swift-water rescues and/or body recoveries per year, and one or two major searches that go on

Afternoon light turns Bridalveil Fall into liquid gold. The 62-story free-falling cascade was known to the Ahwahneechee Indians as Pohono, "Spirit of the Puffing Wind." Winds blowing through the valley can pick up the spray and swirl it about like gossamer veils.

TOURS WITH RANGERS

for more than a day. Fincher crunches the numbers: "The people that we hike down with a sprained knee in a litter, that doesn't cost very much—a few hundred dollars. The climber halfway up El Cap—that might be five or ten thousand dollars. But if you want to talk real money, you take the five-year-old kid who wanders away from the campground and you look for him for a week. You can get up to a hundred or two hundred thousand dollars." Such efforts can involve hundreds of searchers. With the cost of rescues making headlines, Fincher cautions that "it's not as simple as 'Oh, those daredevil climbers going up and doing stupid things and we're spending taxpayers' money to save them.' That's part of it, but that's not the whole picture."

Energetic ranger Shelton Johnson, one of very few African-American rangers in the western national parks, has rediscovered a missing piece of the Yosemite picture that he says is vital for its future. While earning a master of fine arts in poetry from the University of Michigan, he worked summers in the mid-1980s in Yellowstone. One day he took a friend out for a look at the geysers. Everywhere they went, along with admiring the scenery, his friend kept asking, "Where are all the black people?" The question stayed with Johnson over the years. Then, while working at Yosemite, he found a photograph of a black infantry regiment on patrol in the park. No one knew much about them.

Initial research led to more in-depth research, then to a grant to visit several parks. Hundreds of hours among archives has resulted in the story of the Buffalo Soldiers in Yosemite and Sequoia National Parks. In the second half of the 19th century the mostly African-American Ninth and Tenth cavalry regiments—called Buffalo Soldiers by the Indians—helped protect western settlers, fought Indians, and captured outlaws. That they also provided a federal presence in the national parks was largely forgotten until Johnson's work came to light. "There were people in the surrounding community who didn't believe the history had taken place," says Johnson. "It countered the prevailing view of who was in Yosemite a hundred years ago."

More than 200 Buffalo Soldiers served in Yosemite during the turn of the last century, their duties similar to those of today's backcountry mounted rangers. "They were like a police officers walking a beat," says Johnson. They made sure people extinguished their campfires, escorted sheepherders out of the park, and prevented poaching and timber harvesting. "What made it very challenging was that this was a time when African

Simple pleasures of Yosemite come in various guises. Above, a Sierra tiger lily grows in a secluded area of the park called White Wolf. Yosemite's habitats hold more than 1,000 species of wildflowers, 37 varieties of native trees, 150 bird species, 85 mammal species, and 33 kinds of reptiles and amphibians. Below, a visitor soaks up afternoon sun at the historic Wawona Hotel, dating from the late 19th century.

TOURS WITH RANGERS

Americans, along with Native Americans and some immigrant groups, occupied the lowest rung on the social ladder, so it gave their job a little bit more of an edge."

From his research Johnson has created a composite character that he portrays in his frequent Buffalo Soldier walks and theatrical presentations. One thing he asked himself when creating the character was, "Why were most of the soldiers from the Deep South?" After Reconstruction, Jim Crow, and the rise of the Ku Klux Klan, "there were very few opportunities for these folks who wanted to do something other than be a laborer or sharecropper. The military offered a way out."

After several years interpreting the Buffalo Soldiers, Johnson says he's ready to shift back toward natural history, his original passion. One of his favorite things to do is walk in the meadows of Yosemite Valley during a full moon, when everyone's asleep. The lack of light pollution, he says, combined with the reflective quality of the silica in the granite gives the valley walls a magical glow, and Yosemite Falls can cast a brilliant lunar rainbow. The moon reminds him of full moons in Liberia, West Africa, where he worked in the Peace Corps. Full moons there were almost too bright to look at. "In Liberia it really dawned on me how much we've lost because of civilization. We've lost that connection to the primeval night. Indigenous peoples have something that we've lost, and we don't even know we've lost it."

Johnson sees the Buffalo Soldier story primarily as "a hook" for getting more African Americans to visit the park and experience its natural wonders. He has noticed a rise in African-American visitation since he started his Buffalo Soldier program. "If people hear a story that pertains to them and is inclusive of them, then they're more likely to attend. They may not feel a connection with someone like John Muir, who's an iconic figure at Yosemite National Park, but not necessarily for African Americans.

"This situation is something that some folks within the park service, as well as outside, don't perceive as a problem. Yet this is a pluralistic society and it's becoming more pluralistic. Here we are in California, where Euro-Americans are no longer the majority. There's a shift that's happening, and if the park service doesn't keep up with that shift in demographics—if we keep 'preaching to the choir' and not to African Americans, Hispanics, and Asian Americans—if they don't feel a part of the national park experience, then why would they pay money to support it? I am passionate about the parks; I love the experience of being in wilderness areas and I want these parks to continue. In 50 years if there are large populations out there who have not bought into the idea of national parks, there may not be national parks."

Mountains

The quick answer to what makes SEQUOIA and KING'S CANYON NATIONAL PARKS unique, says ranger Bill Tweed, "is that we have the biggest trees in the world and the highest peak in the 48 states, Mount Whitney." But the heart-of-the-matter answer he gives is that these combined parks preserve classic Western wilderness, or what he calls "giant wild landscapes."

A native Californian, Tweed was working on a Ph.D. in history when he discovered that he could be a teacher in the parks, where he was spending his summers. "So I jumped from the "University of Whatever" to the "University of Sequoia," where we teach people about nature." He has been at Sequoia since 1978 and is now chief naturalist.

"We like to say we're the size of a small New England state," Tweed says of the parks. "There's lots of terrain, lots of variety. We have an 800-mile trail system and 1,200 square miles of land, so there's a lot of stuff out there." He heartily recommends the obvious—a walk in the Giant Forest. The three-square-mile plateau sitting at 6,000 feet in the Sierra has the biggest trees in the world. "Some of the best walking in the park is in the Giant Forest, places where you can walk literally one, two, three miles to the most beautiful for-

SEQUOIA NATIONAL PARK

est you can imagine, and often be by yourself even on very busy days." Among the giant sequoias here are such ancients as the approximately 2,000-year-old General Sherman Tree—275 feet tall, 103 feet in circumference.

In Kings Canyon, Tweed suggests going straight to the canyon itself. He likes exploring around Zumwalt Meadow and Road's End. One of his favorite walks here is the Southside Trail to Bubbs Creek, a four-mile loop along the riverbank in the flow of a gigantic glacial gorge lined by 3,000-foot cliffs. John Muir said the area was a rival to Yosemite. "It's another Yosemite," agrees Tweed, "but one with about 5 percent the human use."

For something more ambitious, and "a taste of the high country," Tweed raves about a hike in Mineral King, which lies off a 25-mile side road. The drive itself is something of a challenge—a narrow, winding road climbing to 7,800 feet. At the end of the road, the White Chief Trail takes off at a steep pitch, altogether ascending 2,000 feet in three breathless but thrilling miles. "You're climbing up out of a glacial valley into a basin that is heavily glaciated," says Tweed. "You've got views of high peaks, a zone of marble with high-altitude caves, a historic mine, beautiful timberline foxtail pines, meadows, and wild-flowers in the summer." The tough but highly rewarding climb gives hikers "a sense of what the three-quarters of the park is that's wilderness," says Tweed.

LASSEN VOLCANIC NATIONAL PARK

Up in north-central California, LASSEN VOL-CANIC NATIONAL PARK protects a different kind of mountain landscape. Since its last series of erup-tions, from 1915 to 1921, Lassen has been quiet. But it is still a volcano, the centerpiece of a vast panorama of volcanism—of ruined mountains, devastated land, and bubbling cauldrons of mud.

Ranger Karen Haner, who grew up in nearby Redding, says one of her favorite places in the park is the top of Brokeoff Mountain, a composite volcano some 400,000 years old. The 9,235-foot peak offers even more dramatic views than Lassen Peak itself, she claims, and is less populated. Not only is it a wonderful four-mile hike, it also provides a sterling vantage from which to study volcanism.

In the summer she likes to head down to King Creek Falls, to hear and see the rush-ing water of the cascades. She recently took a film crew there to get footage for a park film. "They spent a lot more time there than they thought they would," she says. "They were upset that I hadn't told them how great it was, and I said, 'Well, I tried.'"

Of the active geothermal areas, Haner is particularly fond of the lesser known Dev-ils Kitchen. Unlike the boardwalks of Bumpass Hell, you walk along paths that are directly in the thermal area. "You get a real sense of the rumbling of the Earth, you hear the steam and the plopping of mud pots. And there's a super-charged vent that almost sounds like a jet taking off." In addition, the air is hot and sulphurous, and if you return at a differ-ent time of year, says Haner, the hot spots may have shifted location.

For a close encounter with lava beds, nothing can beat the trail up Cinder Cone, an almost symmetrical 700-foot-high mound of lava. "I've only hiked it twice in my life," says Haner of the tough climb over loose cinders, "but boy is it worth it once you get up there. The painted dunes are around them and the huge lava flow that came out the base of the cone. It looks so new. It happened around 1650, so it's a recent volcanic event."

Tremendous stone trees lie scattered about the desert floor in Arizona's Petrified Forest National Park. Layered bluffs in the background, at the park's Jasper Forest area, reveal eons of geological history. Fossilized plants and animals litter the park, the result of 200 million years of slow change to the environment.

CHAPTER 2

A Trip
Back in Time

While many parks casually mention ages such as 225 million years, Petrified Forest National Park is one of the few places where you can actually almost see what the landscape was like that long ago. The trees are no longer standing, of course, but many of them lie scattered about, now turned to multi-colored stone. In fact, the park contains one of the highest concentrations of fossilized wood in the world. With giant fallen trees lying all around, it's not a huge leap to imagine the rest of the scene: early dinosaurs, giant ferns, weird crocodilians, spatula-headed amphibians—a humid, jungly, birdless place completely different from today's dry high desert environment.

What many people first consider a casual stop off route I-40 becomes an adventure into the deep past, and a seemingly empty landscape fills with color, texture, and life.

Ranger Marge Post came to Petrified Forest after stints at the Grand Canyon and as a Peace Corps volunteer in Fiji. As an education technician, she takes groups young and old out and explains the landscape. She is adept at opening up compressed layers of history for easy inspection. One of the first things she points out is that the Painted Desert and the Petrified Forest are all one park. The colorful rock layers, she explains, are known as the Chinle Formation and were laid down some 225 million years ago when the area was a low-lying floodplain. Post describes the Painted Desert as a geological wonderland of hues that look like "sunset over the landscape."

The southern part of the park contains the namesake massive quantities of petrified wood. Post lays out the petrification process: "If you have a huge river system coming in here and it's starting to spread out like it does in a floodplain— think of the Mississippi Delta, but ten times bigger—there's a lot of small stuff that comes in—a lot of sand, a lot of silt, a lot of clay, a lot of mud, and a lot of

Creosote bushes and sage plants speckle the Painted Desert near Tiponi Point in the park's north section. Sunsets and thunderstorms, the latter often visible dozens of miles away, draw out the multiple hues of the Painted Desert.

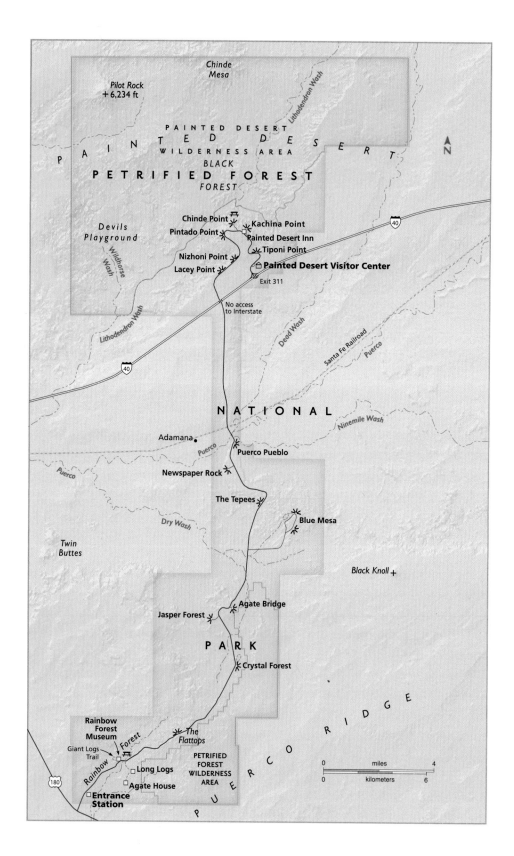

Chinde
Mesa

Pilot Rock
+ 6,234 ft

PAINTED DESERT

P A I N T E D   D E S E R T

WILDERNESS AREA

BLACK

PETRIFIED FOREST

FOREST

Devils
Playground

Wildhorse Wash

Chinde Point

Pintado Point

Kachina Point

Painted Desert Inn

Nizhoni Point

Tiponi Point

Lacey Point

Painted Desert Visitor Center

Exit 311

40

No access
to Interstate

Lithodendron Wash

Lithodendron Wash

Dead Wash

Santa Fe Railroad

Puerco

40

N A T I O N A L

Ninemile Wash

Adamana

Puerco

Puerco Pueblo

Newspaper Rock

The Tepees

Blue Mesa

Dry Wash

Twin
Buttes

Black Knoll +

Agate Bridge

Jasper Forest

P U E R C O   R I D G E

P A R K

Crystal Forest

Rainbow
Forest
Museum

Forest

**The
Flattops**

Giant Logs
Trail

**PETRIFIED
FOREST
WILDERNESS
AREA**

180

Rainbow

☐ **Long Logs**

☐ **Agate House**

☐ **Entrance
Station**

| miles |
| 0 | 4 |
| 0 | 6 |
| kilometers |

Ancient rock art—petroglyphs 650 to 2,000 years old—crowd the surface of Newspaper Rock. Vandalism (notice the missing pieces) and unstable hillsides have led to trail closure, but the rock may be observed with spotting scopes.

volcanic ash." That ash contributed silica to the sediment, which helped petrify the wood and turn it into quartz.

As the ecosystem changed from lush subtropical to the present-day arid semi-desert grassland, the plants and animals living here during the Triassic period were preserved in the soft mudstone and claystone. Thus animal fossils are also prevalent in the park, and Post has learned how to spot an exposed bone. With heavy late summer rains and a freeze-thaw cycle in winter, the local erosion rate is high; once a fossil is exposed, it may begin eroding away within a few years. "The trick to finding those animal fossils is to be really lucky and walk up on them before weathering decays them all away," she says. "I always have it in the back of my head that maybe I will discover that new species." She laughs, but then adds, "You never know, we're averaging two to four new species of plants and vertebrate animals per year."

Among the finds was one that changed the way people view dinosaur evolution.

Park paleontologist Bill Parker was out in the summer of 2004 with some geologists doing a survey of fossil localities. They were in the Painted Desert Wilderness section of the park when Parker noticed an outcrop beside an original river channel. To Parker's experienced eye, the area looked promising for fossils. "It turned out to be very good," says Parker. What they found there was the skeleton of a *Revueltosaurus*. Previously, only the teeth of this ancient reptile had been found, and it was assumed that *Revueltosaurus* was a plant-eating ornithischian dinosaur, one of two main branches of dinosaurs that include *Triceratops* and *Stegosaurus*. "Come to find out," says Parker, "it's not a dinosaur at all—it's a little ancestral crocodile. It had armor plates along the back, similar to plates you find on crocodiles. But the key thing was when we actually found the ankle." In crocodiles the rotation joint is between the two main ankle bones; in dinosaurs the two bones are fused together and the rotation occurs below. "That affects posture—crocodiles are more sprawling, birds and dinosaurs are more upright."

The important thing about the find is that the entire North American record of Triassic ornithischian dinosaurs is based on similar teeth. "So we've basically erased the Triassic ornithischian dinosaur record from everywhere except for South America." Ornithischians possibly originated in South America and radiated everywhere else in the Jurassic. "We were kind of shocked actually," confides Parker.

The finding of so many new species in the park, says Parker, has only occurred since 2001, "when we really kicked the paleo program into gear. It's the result of going out and doing some hard work and hitting the ground." A walk in the park is for Parker never a matter of simply enjoying the scenery. "It's pretty hard to go hiking around here and not think about paleontology. I'm looking for bones, or I'm looking at the geology."

Historic preservationist Amanda Zeman is looking at much more recent history in Petrified Forest National Park. Only a few years out of graduate school, Zeman is the park's "lone ranger" of historic preservation, working to ensure that any changes to existing buildings comply with the National Historic Preservation Act. Many visitors are surprised to find that a park known for its natural history has any historic structures at all. Petrified Forest has several, including a 1950s building that through Zeman's meticulous research and documentation was listed on the National

Balancing act: Erosion continues to expose and gnaw away at pedestal logs in the Blue Mesa area. Long ago the area's trees and other plants were buried in soft mud; some decomposed, others were fossilized. Continental drift then altered the climate from lush tropical to dry desert.

TOURS WITH RANGERS

Keeping an old art alive, a weaver works a loom in the Painted Desert Inn. The National Historic Landmark inn, dating from the 1920s, spotlights the park's 20th-century history. Built of petrified wood and native stone, the inn features Pueblo Revival architecture and floors painted with Navajo designs.

The ruins of Agate House stand in stark surroundings. The eight-room dwelling, possibly constructed entirely of petrified wood, was built about 700 years ago by ancestral Puebloans. A 1930s restoration used concrete to stabilize the walls.

Following pages: Striated badlands dwarf a hiker in Blue Mesa, where multicolored bentonitic clay has eroded into outlandish shapes. Thick deposits of blue, gray, purple, and green mudstones and some sandstone were laid down about 234 million years ago.

Register of Historic Places. But the park's most significant historic building is the Painted Desert Inn, a National Historic Landmark.

Originally constructed around 1924 by Herbert David Lore, the inn was rebuilt in the 1930s by the Civilian Conservation Corps. It was bought by the Fred Harvey Company in the late 1940s and remodeled by noted architect and interior designer Mary Colter. She hired Hopi artist Fred Kabotie to paint several murals of Hopi symbols and ceremonies. "The murals are painted directly on the plaster," says Zeman, "and for the quality of workmanship they are for all intents and purposes irreplaceable." Thus when the inn recently underwent a major rehabilitation it was returned to its 1948 appearance, to preserve the integrity of the murals in their original setting. "We picked that time period primarily because of the murals but also because anywhere along the Old Santa Fe Railroad, the Fred Harvey

Company had a very active presence in the national parks and a very signature architectural style."

Zeman says the Painted Desert Inn is her favorite place in the park. "It's kind of a magical place because it sits right on the edge of the Painted Desert. If you're there close to dawn or dusk, the Painted Desert glows with many different colors. The Painted Desert Inn was designed to enhance that experience—the color of the stucco matches the Painted Desert. It's done in a Pueblo Revival style, so if you look at that scene through the lens of a camera there's all kinds of dramatic views that have the building in the foreground, the Painted Desert in the background." Zeman especially likes the inn's quietness and the sense it gives of removal to a slower paced lifestyle. When the inn reopens as a museum in fall 2005 it will feature original furniture, light fixtures, mirrors, handpressed tinware, and hand-painted skylights.

Another surprising aspect of Petrified Forest National Park is the abundant prehistoric human presence. Hundreds of archaeological sites lie scattered throughout the 94,000-acre park. Although the park has no full-time archaeologist, Scott Williams, curator of the park's Rainbow Forest Museum, is an enthusiastic spokesman for the park's wealth of both archaeology and paleontology.

Before coming to the park four years ago, Williams was a photographer for the Smithsonian Institution's National Museum of American History in Washington, D.C. Having gone to school in the Southwest he wondered, "Am I going to be kicking myself ten years down the road for not getting back out here?" So he and his girlfriend got married and moved out, thinking they'd be here for a year or two. But the place has proved harder to leave than he imagined. In addition to doing research photography in the museum and the field, he has been of invaluable assistance to visiting botanists, entomologists, archaeologists, vertebrate paleontologists, graduate students, and a host of other researchers. "There's never a dull moment," he says.

The museum itself is one of the park's highlights. Of the 200,000 objects in the collection, about 500 or so are on display at any given time. In addition to dioramas of ancient environments and exhibits of vertebrate and invertebrate fossils from the Triassic, the museum displays pre-Columbian artifacts made from, among other substances, petrified wood.

People have lived in the region for nearly 10,000 years, leaving traces of their existence. There is a particularly high concentration of artifacts dating from A.D. 950-1300 from the ancestral Pueblo people who lived here. Among their tools were stone manos and metates (used for grinding grains), petrified wood and obsidian points and scrapers, and local and trade-good pottery. The park also holds thousands of petroglyph panels—symbols and designs scratched, pecked, or carved onto rock walls—dating from 650 to 2,000 years ago.

A close-up look at lichen-striped petrified wood can reveal details kept intact for millions of years. Buried in soft mud, some logs were then blanketed by windblown ash from western volcanoes Silica leached from the ash and bit by bit replaced the trees' cells with quartz crystals; iron and other minerals added color.

Some of these archeological sites lie just off the park road. The eight-room Agate House was built of petrified wood and adobe by ancestral Puebloans more than 800 years ago; a 1930s reconstruction used concrete to stabilize the walls. Puerco Pueblo village, abandoned about 1380, contains numerous well-preserved petroglyphs of animals and geometric designs. One chiseled circle likely served as a solar calendar—a shaft of sunlight hits the center on the summer solstice.

Other sites lie farther afield, beyond the road and trails. For security reasons, Williams prefers not to divulge specific details about these amazing sites. Suffice it to say that in numerous places one can come across pottery sherds and other artifacts lying on the ground right where they have been for a thousand years. "You'll go out into the backcountry and find a lithic scatter or ceramic scatter in most areas of the park," he says. "That's one of the hidden secrets of this park, there's still so much out here. This isn't southern Utah or the Grand Canyon—people aren't drawn to this park because it's a thousand feet of vertical rock or something like that."

The beauty of Petrified Forest, Williams suggests, is more subtle. He cites Blue Mesa, in the middle of the park, as one of his favorite areas. A trail through here winds through weird badlands banded in purple, blue, and cream colors that alter with weather and time of day.

Williams speaks perhaps most fondly of the Painted Desert Wilderness, which comprises some 50,000 acres in the north part of the park. He compares the multicolored landscape to that of Mars or some other planet. From 6,234-foot Pilot Rock, the highest point in the park, the panorama is vast and compelling. But even from a place like Pintado Point, just off the road, on a clear day you can see all the way to Flagstaff, 120 miles to the west. And you can watch storms piling up from miles away during the late summer monsoon season.

"I remember one August, the second year I was out here," Williams recalls. "I was taking photographs trying to capture the emotion of one of these storms coming over the Painted Desert. I was set up at Kachina Point. Sitting there with an older four-by-five camera with a big tripod, you're pretty much a lightning rod. But I felt that this was something visitors should experience. I watched this huge thunderhead coming in from the west and just erupting onto the Painted Desert Wilderness area, and I was able to shoot two sheets of film and then run back to the Painted Desert Inn, where I took refuge in the basement taproom. It was just lightning, thunder, dust flying, and a wall of water."

The most beautiful part was yet to come. "After about five or ten minutes the storm blew out and I went back out to Kachina Point, and now the sun was illuminating all the bentonitic clay hills that are deep reds and pinks and oranges, with some whites

Fourteenth-century desert condo living: The ruins of Puerco Pueblo reveal a dwelling of more than one hundred one-story rooms, constructed around a rectangular plaza near the Puerco River. Ceremonies were held in three kivas—circular underground rooms. By about A.D. 1400 the site had been abandoned, its remaining occupants likely moving to larger communities.

for contrast. With all that rain soaking into the clay, it was just an amazing saturation of color. That's when I made another shot toward the east where the rains had passed over, and with the contrast of the dark clouds it was one of the best images of the monsoons that I'd ever taken here or anywhere in the West....I grew up near Chicago and we had storms, but the humidity dampens everything out. There's nothing like smelling the rain out here when it hits the air."

One of Williams's favorite things to do in the park is go out on expeditions with a man he calls the Petrified Forest backcountry guru. Nearing 65, ranger Ted Bolich has led an adventurous life that includes 20 years as a geologist and prospector. Deserts have been his chosen landscape. He was born and raised on the Atacama Desert of northern Chile, went to college in the Chihuahuan Desert in El Paso, Texas, then worked as an exploration geologist in Mexico's Sonoran Desert, prospecting for gold, silver, copper, lead, and zinc. For a while he had a job in an open-pit copper mine in Peru, but found it boring. "It was just shift changes and moving shovels and dump trucks and trains around." After a stint teaching math and science in Holbrook, Arizona, he began working for Petrified Forest in 1988 and has been here for a six-month season ever since, with one year out for a hip replacement.

His years as a prospector gave him a love for the open wilderness and for maps. "I can go out in any kind of environment," he says, "preferably a desert. I feel very comfortable with topographic maps and a compass. I'm not a GPS geologist, although I carry a GPS unit on my pack in case I find something important—I can take the GPS reading back to the researchers."

When asked if he knows every square foot of the park, Bolich chuckles in agreement. Still, he says there are a few little corners that he hasn't covered, places where he needs "to get out and prospect a little bit." And even after 17 years he finds the park fascinating. "There's just so much to entertain you out there—petroglyphs, ruins, pottery sherds, petrified wood, the occasional coyote or pronghorn....My wife keeps saying to me, look, you promised when you retired from school you were going to do other parks, and I keep coming back to Petrified Forest. I haven't seen everything there is to see here, probably won't in a lifetime."

One quiet area Bolich finds especially attractive is the Devils Playground, in the southwestern corner of the Painted Desert Wilderness. "The landforms are so intriguing, it's almost like an alien world—all the little sculpted hoodoo formations

Sunset illuminates a petroglyph panel, scratched or pecked into the stone hundreds of years ago. Symbols, anthropomorphic figures, and animals may represent clans or have an association with fertility and hunting rituals. Many of these ancient designs have found their way into modern Hopi and Zuni artwork.

down there. There's a little bit of bone material and a few petroglyphs that I still haven't seen." He also favors the Pilot Rock area to the north. The shiny black basalt of Pilot Rock forms a backdrop for a tremendous variety of lichens. "There was a thesis done by a lichens expert from Phoenix," says Bolich, "and we have over 100 kinds of lichens described at Petrified Forest, of which 12 to 16 occur only here." In one small four-foot-square section of Pilot Rock, Bolich himself identified nine different lichens, varying in color from florescent yellow to light green.

There is nothing about the park that does not interest Bolich. "You can go out after hard rains and enjoy the plant life, and you can look up at a backdrop of badlands hills, showing mesas and buttes, and all the colors of the layers. You could be walking across a nothing landscape of sand dunes and all at once you're crossing a fairly tall dune and it'll have a blowout on one side—a side that's been eroded completely—and out in the middle there may be a rock, and you'll go up and turn the rock over and it's a metate (grinding stone). And at the top of the dunes there's pottery sherds and sandstone slabs where somebody built some kind of a home."

Bolich likes to hike out about eight miles into the backcountry, drop his pack, then trek back to his car and load up with big canteens and water bladders—all the water he'll need for two or three days. With a base established, he can "prospect" the desert to his heart's content, even in 100-degree weather so arid it can dry wet clothes in 15 minutes. "People laugh at me, I love it so much." He adds sadly, "And the people that don't go out and take advantage of the backcountry, I say, well, it's your loss, there's just so much out there to see. Everybody that goes out, they come back so happy, so satisfied. It's soul-searching, harsh country."

Bolich and Williams have teamed up on many expeditions out into the backcountry, and they have a high regard for each other. "We almost have an unwritten language between us," says Bolich. "We'll stop and we'll see a landform that may be a mile or a mile and a half away, and we kind of look at each other, we both nod our heads, and then here we go. I've learned so much about photography just watching him. He said, 'Ted, probably at least 60 percent of all the stuff that we've made into magnets, postcards, posters, and so forth, you were by my side, you took me out there.' The year I had my hip replaced I tried getting him maps and telling him how to get to places, but it's a lot different when you've got somebody to walk you right out there."

If Bolich only has a few more corners of the park to explore, he'll soon have another lifetime's worth of prospecting ahead of him. Recent legislation authorized the expansion of Petrified Forest National Park to 225,000 acres—more than twice its current size. The majority of the lands picked for the expansion were chosen due to their potential for paleontological resources.

Parched mud shrinks and cracks in the Painted Desert, hindering plant growth and leading to erosion.
Heavy summer rains are the main contribution to erosion—gullies etched in the clay carry off up to a
quarter inch of rock from area slopes. Each desert scene tells its own long and involved story.

Petrified logs in the Long Logs area, the highest concentration of petrified wood in the park, measure up to 120 feet in length. Tumbled and abraded by floods and mudflows, the fallen trees washed into logjams. Woodgrain, knotholes, and beetle borings are often rendered in fine detail by the stone.

The entire area, maintains Marge Post, is rich in paleontological and archaeological sites. "We estimate that we protect only about 10 percent of all the petrified wood deposits in the whole area." Beyond the current park boundaries, a couple of big landowners, in line to sell to the park, have "been very good about protecting the resources that are out there."

Resource protection has long been a big concern in and around the park. The abundance of the petrified wood has over the years made it an easy target for souvenir hunters. The local Navajo, who considered the logs the bones of the monster Yietso, could not understand the pilfering of petrified wood to decorate home mantelpieces. When a team came to collect logs for the Smithsonian, the Indians "thought it strange the 'Great Father in Washington' should want some of the bones of the 'great giant' their forefathers had killed when taking possession of the country."

With so much petrified wood lying about, many visitors find the temptation to pocket some too hard to resist. Other, more profit-minded individuals manage to haul out large chunks of the wood, which weighs 169 pounds per cubic foot. The theft continues at the rate of over 24,000 pounds every year.

Post believes that education is the key to slowing that rate. "It's not just the petrified wood itself," she says. "If you take a piece and hold it in your hand it's a neat fossil—if you put it on your shelf it's still a neat fossil, but it's out of context. The sheer amount that we have and where it's found and in which layers it's found tells us a lot about the past." She encourages people, if they must take some away, to visit the gift shop and buy wood collected from private lands. And there are even "some public lands where if people understand the rules they can go collect it themselves, and it's the exact same thing."

The park has a big pile of what it calls "conscience wood." Visitors who took petrified wood out of the park will often send it back with apologetic letters, many of which relate the bad luck brought by the stolen artifacts. Some 600 pounds of petrified wood is returned annually by guilt-stricken visitors. Post uses the "conscience wood" during ranger talks, but "the problem is we can't actually return it to the place where they took it from."

Besides simply telling visitors why it's not good to take the wood, Post and the other rangers at Petrified Forest educate by the example of their positive attitude. Their love for the Painted Desert, the layers of geological history, the rich paleontology and archaeology, the summer storms in a brooding landscape—all of it ripples out beyond the borders of the park. Post says that her favorite experiences are working with students: "Having a group of fourth graders come in and seeing the light bulb go on, seeing them finally get it. This is more than just something they've read about; they're really seeing it and they understand that this is an ancient ecosystem that they're looking at. And getting the thank-you letters back or the surveys and seeing that it did click—that makes me feel really good and that I've created a future steward for our national parks."

Deserts

When First Lady Laura Bush visited DEATH VALLEY NATIONAL PARK in March 2005, ranger Charlie Callagan took her to Fall Canyon, one of his favorite places; the 35-foot dryfall is but one of the area's spectacular desert wilderness features. The park was abloom with wildflowers, and the First Lady ended up staying in the park nearly three days, relaxing and hiking with friends and taking part in the National Park Foundation meeting.

For the past 15 years Callagan has tramped and guided visitors over what is now the largest national park south of Alaska. Says Callagan, "The extremes here are unique. It's the hottest, driest, lowest place in the country. You have that combination of the starkness of the land around you—the harsh hot desert—and then the great scenic beauty of the vistas and the mountains that you can see 50 or 100 miles away." With a mere 1.96 inches of annual rainfall, the air is sparkling clear even in summer, when temperatures can rise to 130 degrees.

Geologically speaking, Death Valley is a vast graben, a sunken piece of the Earth's crust. The landscape is one of eroded rocks, richly tinted mudstone hills and canyons, lush oases, luminous sand dunes, and a 200-square-mile salt pan surrounded by mountains that soar to 11,000 feet—one of the country's greatest vertical rises. In some years spring rains trigger lavish wildflower blooms amid more than a thousand varieties of plants.

DEATH VALLEY NATIONAL PARK

"You should not miss the classic scenic viewpoints of the badlands," urges Callagan. He mentions Zabriskie Point, a promontory commanding wide views of mudstone badlands, as a viewing spot for sunsets. A fine place for early morning photography, says Callagan, is Badwater, which is also the lowest point in the Western Hemisphere at 282 feet below sea level.

For both sunsets and sunrises, Callagan likes Stovepipe Wells, to the north. The sand dunes there, made of quartz fragments, have no established trails, so people wander at will. It's a good area for exploring, says Callagan, unless there's a wind.

Callagan started out in Death Valley as a seasonal ranger, but for the past eight years he has stayed on through the harsh summer months. "Most of us who are here in the summer love the heat, but that doesn't mean it doesn't get too extreme even for us." He and other rangers like to get away into the cooler mountains when they can. Summer visitation, he says, is mostly European tourists on their way between Las Vegas and Yosemite. "Death Valley is a short stop for them in the summer to experience the heat a bit. It's not safe to do much hiking in the lower valley in the summer."

Another regular getaway for Callagan are his shopping trips. Some people settle for the stores in a town called Pahrump, about 60 miles away, but Callagan prefers to drive an extra 60 miles to Las Vegas. The contrast between total isolation and total glitter must be worth the trip.

JOSHUA TREE NATIONAL PARK

South of Death Valley, JOSHUA TREE NATIONAL PARK straddles the transition zone between two desert environments. On the east side, the Colorado or "low desert" thrives below 3,000 feet elevation; the Mojave ("high desert") ecosystem claims the western half of the park, where a wetter environment produces such distinctive vegetation as the Joshua tree, a giant branching yucca.

Ranger Joe Zarki, the park's chief of interpretation, likes a high perspective in the middle of the park from which to view the whole thing. The strenuous but not long hike up to the 5,461-foot peak of Mount Ryan gives one a sense of the large scale of the park and its dual desert landscapes. The 360-degree views also provides a view of smog creeping over the edge of the mountains from a Land of Mordor 140 miles west known as Los Angeles.

Another of Zarki's favorite hikes is the easier but longer trek to Lost Palms Oasis on the east side of the park. The largest of Joshua Tree's five native palm oases, Lost Palms is "peaceful, shady, and very remote." It provides a bit of coolness from the desert heat and a chance to spot orioles, hummingbirds, and other wildlife. "Occasionally during dry periods you may see bighorn sheep coming down to these oases to get water," says Zarki.

In addition to dramatic desert views, wildlife, and some 19th-century gold mine ruins, one growing attraction in the park is the night sky. "More and more of our visitors are coming out just because they can't see stars in L.A. and other urban communities," says Zarki. "The skies here are still clear, but that could change over time as development increases in southern California. That's one of the take-home messages we like to point out: Take a look at what you've got here and think about what we can do to hang onto it."

Laying a golden trail across Lake Superior, the departing sun burnishes islands near Rock Harbor at Isle Royale National Park. The remote 45-mile-long island lies several hours by boat from mainland Michigan and Minnesota, making it the least visited of all national parks.

CHAPTER 3

Quiet Island Sanctuary

T hat Isle Royale is the least visited of all the national parks has little to do with its natural beauty. On the 45-mile-long island, wolves and moose coexist in a predator-prey symbiosis, loon calls echo on foggy mirror-smooth lakes, bald eagles survey their kingdoms from ancient trees, and industrious beavers alter the environment far more than man. A wonderfully wild world of rocky shores, shadowy bogs, and high ridges, the island holds an abundance of pristine beauty. What keeps visitation low is the park's remoteness. Stranded in Lake Superior off the northernmost reaches of Minnesota and Michigan, Isle Royale lies nearly within Canadian waters. Visitors who make the drive to the nearest mainland ports still have a three- to six-hour ferry ride ahead of them. To make it worth the time, most people plan to stay a few days.

"The remoteness is what grows on you," says veteran ranger Larry Kangas in his weathered voice. Having spent 15 years at Isle Royale—25 total at parks in the region—he knows the allure of the lake lifestyle. "It's more simple, you're not running around in a vehicle. You throw your wallet in a drawer when you get here because you're not spending a lot of money other than maybe a mail order here or there. It's a place where the sounds of nature prevail."

When asked what one should do with two days to spend at Isle Royale, Kangas answers, "You're probably selling yourself a little short. It takes two days just to come and go." His advice is to plan on a longer stay. Yet for those who want a glimpse of the island, Kangas suggests coming to Rock Harbor on the east end, where a variety of developed trails offers chances to spot a moose or fox and get a feel for "the island quiet and solitude."

On the west end, only 20 miles of water separate the island from Minnesota's mainland (compared with more than twice that distance from Michigan's Copper Harbor to Isle Royale's Rock Harbor). This is where the 5,000 annual day-use visitors embark. "They get about three hours to spend on small trails," says Kangas, "a ranger

Purple iris adorns a sunny bog on Raspberry Island, near the park's Rock Harbor. A boreal forest of white spruce, balsam fir, paper birch, and aspen covers this tiny island and Isle Royale.

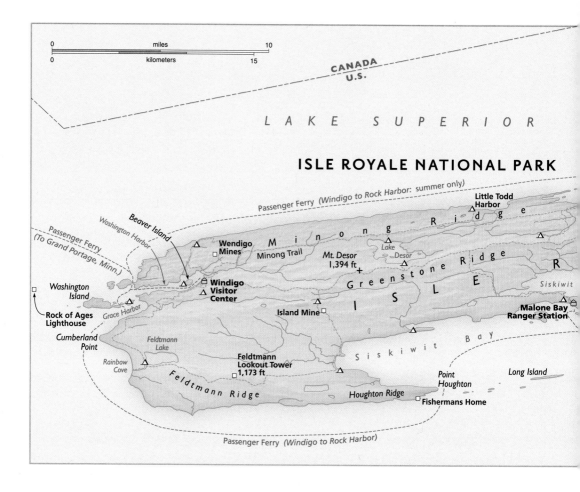

ISLE ROYALE NATIONAL PARK

Passenger Ferry (Windigo to Rock Harbor: summer only)

Little Todd Harbor

Washington Harbor

Beaver Island

Passenger Ferry (To Grand Portage, Minn.)

Wendigo Mines

Minong Trail

M i n o n g

R i d g e

Lake Desor

Mt. Desor 1,394 ft

G r e e n s t o n e

R i d g e

Windigo Visitor Center

Washington Island

Rock of Ages Lighthouse

Grace Harbor

Island Mine

I S L E

Siskiwit

R

Malone Bay Ranger Station

Cumberland Point

Feldtmann Lake

S i s k i w i t

B a y

Rainbow Cove

Feldtmann Lookout Tower 1,173 ft

F e l d t m a n n

R i d g e

Houghton Ridge

Point Houghton

Long Island

Fishermans Home

Passenger Ferry (Windigo to Rock Harbor)

L A K E   S U P E R I O R

CANADA
U.S.

0 ——— miles ——— 10
0 ——— kilometers ——— 15

program, and what they can see from the boat coming and going. You can see historic lighthouses and fisheries, and of course miles of uninterrupted shoreline." The ferry ride in itself makes a good segue to the island, says Kangas: "You get out in the middle of the lake and you don't see any land and you wonder what you're getting into. Then on the way back it provides adequate time to think about your trip before you have to readjust to the mainland."

Visitors who overnight on the island are generally serious about backpacking, fishing, canoeing, or kayaking. Many will ferry around the island to a desired dock, then head off into the interior, which is speckled with some 40 named lakes as well as a number of other smaller lakes. The ones without campsites are especially appealing to Kangas. Canoeing from lake to lake requires portaging—with distances ranging from a tenth of a mile to two miles, over terrain that can vary from soupy to steep and rocky. Those in good enough shape get a quality experience commensurate with the work they put into it.

Kangas particularly likes Isle Royale in fall—the leaves are in full color; the moose are in rut, with antlers fully developed; there are few bugs; and the little bit of tourism

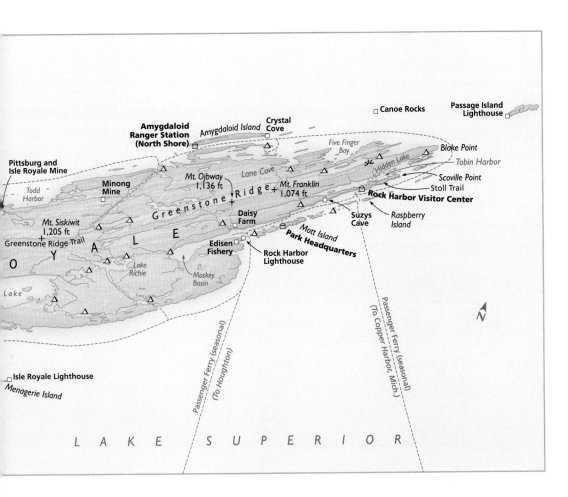

has fallen to a trickle. This is when the island is most fully itself. But, he says, "you want to be out before the gales of November start blowing and the sea conditions become hazardous." In fact, the park is closed from November through March, with ice conditions usually dictating the exact closing and reopening dates.

The only winter use of Isle Royale is the annual wolf-moose study. Kangas generally returns for a couple of weeks to help with the population surveys, which are carried out by plane and on the ground. The study is one of the world's longest running wildlife research projects. Since 1958 biologists have been monitoring moose and wolves—many of them fitted with radio collars—in winter, when they are easiest to spot. Biologists believe moose first swam to the island in the early 1900s; with no natural predators their numbers soared by the 1920s to as many as 3,000. During the bitter winter of 1948-49 an ice bridge formed from Ontario to Isle Royale, allowing a small pack of wolves to cross to the island. The wolves thrived on the plentiful moose. And so began an interdependent cycle. With a large moose herd, wolves prevent overpopulation by culling the sick, the old, and the young. The wolf population peaked at about 50 animals in 1970, but the number had dropped to 14 by 1998—meanwhile, moose numbers rose.

Being a ranger in a remote wilderness park is not all about communing with nature. Among the challenges Kangas cites are the concerns some visitors have with the definition of wilderness. Some prefer a wilder experience than others. "The Lake Superior areas that surround us are non-wilderness," he explains. "Powerboaters are permitted, but a lot of the areas that they use—the docks and campgrounds—are wilderness. And so you have an area where those two zones meet, and two different user groups with different expectations." For many years there were complaints that boaters were coming in and ruining the peace and quiet, but Kangas says that with higher fuel prices and more education those complaints have slowed. A new backcountry management plan seeks to more clearly define what will be allowed where.

Another constant challenge to Isle Royale rangers are the many search-and-rescue missions. "It's a big lake," says Kangas, "offering all kinds of weather, large waves, and sometimes zero visibility with the fog." Simply getting to a location to help somebody can prove problematic, then bad weather can compound the difficulty in getting the victim of a serious incident off to a mainland hospital. For a helicopter to respond to a call, fly in, and evacuate someone to the hospital takes a minimum of three hours. If helicopters cannot fly in, a boat must be used, meaning considerable delay. Kangas estimates that the park has about 60 medical instances a year, with about 6 requiring evacuation; in addition, there are some dozen search and rescues per year.

Ranger Kyle McDowell, who grew up on Lake Erie, also has a lot to say about "medicals," or medical emergencies. "Since we're isolated out here, most of us are EMTs or paramedics," he says. He is an EMT, an emergency medical technician. He recently helped evacuate a woman who fell on a sharp stick and may have punctured her eyeball. Another visitor had a swelling of the leg that could have indicated an arterial occlusion. After consulting with doctors over the telephone, the rangers decided that the safest course was to get the person to a hospital. Other years they've flown people out for anything from strokes to heart attacks to diving-related injuries, fractures, and dislocations.

"There's a lot of ways to hurt yourself here," says McDowell, "but it's really a more gentle wilderness than many of the big western parks in that we don't have the huge walls and cliffs that people tend to fall off of. The water's cold enough that we don't have a lot of swimming, so we don't see the drownings that other parks might see."

Some 400 small islands rim Isle Royale, including these rocky islands near Rock Harbor (above). A sea-plane (below) splashes down in Rock Harbor, eastern gateway to the park, offering a much faster—if more expensive—ride from Houghton, Michigan, than the 4.5-hour trip by ferry.

TOURS WITH RANGERS

Its velvet antlers dripping, a moose swims across Hidden Lake. Moose did not populate Isle Royale until the early 1900s, when a few likely swam the 20 miles from the mainland. Wolves, their only local predator, crossed on an ice bridge. Powerful swimmers, moose can sustain a six-mile-per-hour pace for two hours.

The water at the surface on a warm summer day might reach the low 60s. But at a hundred feet deep the temperature stays in the high 30s. This is where a lesser known park activity takes place. With visibility of 25 to 50 feet, the lake's crystalline waters are perfect for scuba diving on the island's ten major shipwrecks. Most people prefer dry suits, which are bulkier than wet suits but—by sealing water out—a lot warmer. One of McDowell's most pleasant duties is to don a dry suit and dive down to check on mooring buoys and make sure nothing's been pilfered off the wrecks.

Indeed, one of the things McDowell likes best about his job at Isle Royale is that he can be something of a generalist. At Yosemite, Grand Canyon, and other big parks where he has worked, he found himself more involved in law enforcement than he wanted to be. "Isle Royale doesn't have all the problems that the big western parks have. It's a much quieter place; it's almost like going back in time. We only get 15,000 to 17,000 visitors a year here, and I would see that many people times two in a day in Yosemite Valley.... Isle Royale's got a beauty all its own and a presence that's every bit as powerful as those [more famous] places."

Here, his day starts from his base at the north shore ranger station on Amygdaloid Island. He might take a boat and patrol the campgrounds from Little Todd Harbor out to Blake Point, the island's eastern tip, a span of about 20 miles. "We'll go out to those campgrounds, talk to campers, see how things are going, check permits, check fishing licenses." At dive sites, he checks dive permits. The law enforcement McDowell does is usually a matter of telling people not to soap up in the lakes, leave trash behind, build illegal fires, or catch fish below the legal size. "I don't consider myself in the business to catch people doing things wrong and punish them for it. I'm here to try to encourage them to love the place so much that they'll do the right thing even when the rangers aren't watching."

But if he didn't feel like going out in his powerboat, McDowell could take out a sea kayak, or he could decide to go on backcountry patrol for a few days. He often does this during peak season—late July through early August—to make sure all's well in overflowing campgrounds. Another job he enjoys taking on is wildland fire control. Rangers take turns on a call-out list—when their names are "on the board" they may be called to fight fires out West. "When western fires get to be pretty active, they start requesting resources from all around the country," McDowell explains. "Occasionally we'll have fires on the island itself, but usually they're small."

When he gets a chance to go out and explore the island, McDowell has a number of favorite places. One is the Minong Trail on the western end of the island. "It's our most primitive trail, and probably the most challenging. You might have

On tranquil Lake Richie, a paddler pulls his gear from his canoe after a long day. Lake Richie sits in a chain of some 16 lakes and portages that allow canoeists to travel from the south side of Isle Royale to the north. But the work can be tough, with portages up to two miles long over steep, hilly terrain.

Following pages: Long, narrow, fjord-like Washington Harbor greets visitors to the western side of Isle Royale. The ferry Wenonah *makes the trip from Grand Portage, Minnesota, in three hours, the shortest from any port serving the park.*

to walk across a beaver dam or a log instead of a bridge. And then the trail tends to get up on rocky ridges that are just solid bedrock." He describes a special place where the trail cuts through several miles of deciduous forest—yellow birch, white birch, and maple—which eventually yields to an area that he calls the Place Where the White Pine First Appear. "You're on the edge of a cliff face, and at the

bottom there's a beaver pond. Then all along the cliff there's lots of old weathered, twisted-looking white pines that look like something out of an Oriental scroll painting." Some are rare old-growth white pines that measure up to 13 feet in circumference.

McDowell especially likes crossing the meadow below the beaver pond and climbing a hill on the other side of the cliff to view the afternoon sun on the cliff face. "If you go there in October it's just beautiful. One time I was sitting over there, and a giant bull moose appeared out of nowhere. Usually you hear a bull moose coming. It was huge and had tawny-colored antlers with the light on them, and he was just staring right over at me across the valley, smelling the air trying to figure out what I was. And, as quick as he appeared, he was gone. It's things like that—little moments that aren't spectacular, but you never forget."

There are also places with long views that McDowell has tucked away in his memory. For example, on the eastern end of Greenstone Ridge—the spine of the island—Mount Franklin rises to 1,074 feet—making it 474 feet above the lake's surface. McDowell likes to run up to the ridge from Lane Cove on a steep, zigzagging trail. "Then you finally get up on the Greenstone Ridge, and you can sit on a rock outcropping and look out over the whole North Shore and much of the Canadian shoreline off toward Thunder Bay. On a real clear day it's amazing. You just can't believe there's wildness like that east of the Mississippi River."

Other places for fabulous views are the island's many fire towers. Some, such as the Mount Ojibway tower, are no longer used for spotting fires but have air pollution control monitors and radio repeaters for communication. McDowell describes the view from up top: "On some nights as the sun sets, the moon's rising on the opposite side, and you can watch several lighthouses around the island and along the north shore of Canada start blinking. And then as the sky gets darker the stars start appearing. If you stay late enough in the season you might start seeing the Northern Lights, and then it's just magical and you sit there and say to yourself, 'What a cosmos!' It's quite incredible."

Though Isle Royale is noted for its wilderness, it has a long human history, the remnants of which are part of the island's charm. More than 1,500 copper-mining pits attest to a prehistoric Indian presence dating back at least 4,500 years. The relics of 19th-century loggers and fishermen—buildings, diggings, and roads—are mostly vanishing into the mossy forest. The Edisen Fishery near the Rock Harbor Lighthouse still operates as a living history demonstration of local commercial fishing. And two septuagenarians still practice gillnet fishing—fish swim into the net and get their heads stuck in the mesh;

Since 1908 the Rock of Ages Lighthouse (above) has guarded the west end of Isle Royale. A museum at the
Rock Harbor Lighthouse (below) displays an early beacon. Erected in 1855 to guide ore ships, the lighthouse
closed in 1859 when the mines shut down but reopened between 1874 and 1879 during a second mining venture.

Picnicking on the rocks, hikers take in the island's beauty and solitude from Mount Franklin. One of many high perches on the Greenstone Ridge—the island's 40-mile-long backbone—Mount Franklin tops out at 1,074 feet, high enough for fine views of Isle Royale and Lake Superior. The island's highest point, 1,394-foot Mount Desor, rises farther west on the ridge.

their gills prevent them from backing out. Michigan, which retains fishing jurisdiction around Isle Royale, has mostly outlawed gillnets in favor of the more selective trapnets, which keep fish alive.

The old-timers on Isle Royale have a quota of lake trout they can catch, plus all the whitefish they want, in return for some basic record-keeping on growth rate and population for the state's department of natural resources, which is trying to establish a self-sustaining population of lake trout. As in the old days, the ferry (formerly the supply boat) comes by and picks up the fish and drops off ice for the next haul.

McDowell says that listening to the fishermen's stories brings the past to vivid life. "They have spent their lives here, and they're full of knowledge of the place." What happens when they go? "We all kind of hold our breath, because if they go away I'm not sure it'll be continued. Some of their grandchildren come out and help them fish a little in the fall, but it's not extremely profitable, so I don't think it's something that'll ever come back like it was."

How the fishermen live sets an example that McDowell believes could solve many problems. "They live real simple—they don't have electricity, they don't have running water. They have no telephones, but they have marine radios so they can talk to the *Voyageur II*, a ferry boat that brings out visitors but also brings supplies for island folk. They live in simple cabins, and when those cabins start to fall apart they're going back to the earth. They're not made out of things that are going to be there forever; they're made out of things of the island."

Having worked at Isle Royale in the early 1970s, ranger Carl Terhaar has an even older connection to the past. When he speaks of the old-time commercial fishermen he knew, he's talking about a generation earlier. One fisherman was the father of one of the current old-timers. After a four-year stint on Isle Royale, Terhaar spent 25 years with the Michigan Department of Natural Resources, retired with full benefits and returned to Isle Royale five years ago. Now only 56, he says, in his clipped upper Midwestern accent, the park "fits the bill for what I'm after right now." He's also "a good deal for the park service—they don't have to pay me benefits or health insurance or retirement."

TOURS WITH RANGERS

Hungry backpackers at Daisy Farm Campground fuel up before hitting the trail up to 1,136-foot Mount Ojibway, where mushrooms and other hidden gems (opposite) may spend their entire lives unglimpsed by human eyes. Atop the mountain stands a lookout tower and a solar-powered air-monitoring station.

Terhaar and McDowell share the two-man ranger station on the North Shore; each has a one-bedroom apartment. Terhaar works for about five months, with occasional visits from his wife and grown children, so "there's a lot of opportunity for solitude." But he likes it that way. He is an avid photographer and video shooter, and an occasional fisherman. Above all, he loves being out on the water. "The North Shore where I work has lots of islands, small harbors, and bays scattered all over the place, and great rocky shorelines. The shorelines really stand out to me, and a lot of the backpackers hiking the interior don't get to see them."

He likes to take out an 18-foot outboard boat, his kayak aboard, then go paddling around places like Locke Point, Five Finger Bay, and Todd Harbor on the northeast shore. On the south shore, he favors Chippewa Harbor, a narrow arm of a harbor girded by rocky hills; like many of Isle Royale's harbors, it is a designated quiet/no-wake zone.

As a photographer, Terhaar has a good sense of where the wildlife is. McCargoe Cove has often been a prime spot for moose—they feed on the aquatic vegetation at the shallow end of the cove. The moose population, says Terhaar, has dropped in recent years, likely because of winter ticks. "Enough infestation on a thousand-pound moose makes him weak from loss of blood. With thousands of ticks on him, even a prime age moose is more susceptible to wolf predation." Tick infestations vary depending upon the spring melt. Ticks, dropping off in April, die if they land in snow, but lay eggs if they land on dry ground; the following winter then usually bodes ill for the moose.

But the main thing people want to see, says Terhaar, are the island's elusive wolves. He has seen them only twice. The first time, he and a wolf nearly collided on a trail, startling them both. "The wolf hightailed it in the opposite direction before I could even get the camera up to my eye." But recently he was lucky enough to observe wolves feeding on a moose carcass over a three-hour period.

Terhaar knows of no man-wolf encounters that have resulted in any injuries on the island. But he did hear an amusing wolf story recently. "This spring a couple of campers were camping on Chickenbone Lake early in the season. They had just been down to the lake with a collapsible bucket of water. They came up to their campsite and set the bucket down and went into their tent. Two minutes later they heard this lapping sound. They looked out of the tent and there was a wolf drinking out of their water bucket. They sat and watched for like five minutes. Eventually it ran off with the water bucket and was tossing it up in the air like a dog with a play toy."

As for other wildlife, one of the most commonly heard voices is that of the loon.

The island reclaims one of its own, as lichen and other plants take over a grave in the park. With little human presence in the area, the cycle of decay and regrowth continues at a brisk pace, soon covering all evidence of man's limited enterprise here.

TOURS WITH RANGERS

*Capturing the spirit of the island, a floating artist puts himself at a good vantage for landscape painting.
Sky, water, rocky islands, an echoing loon's cry, and the shifting colors of daylight appeal to the deepest
creative impulse, calling visitors to examine the timeless mysteries of wide open wilderness.*

"This is the only place on the Great Lakes where they actually nest," says Terhaar. "They're more likely to be on smaller inland lakes. A lot of the protected bays and harbors here give some good nesting locations. We've also got a good population of bald eagles. They're quite common to see. And a few owls."

An island wilderness teeming with wildlife is what sets Isle Royale apart from all other national parks. Yet the true wilderness, argues Kyle McDowell, is the lake. "The lake is fairly tranquil most of the summer," he says, "but in the spring and fall all bets are off. Nature bats last out here, and the lake becomes a powerful force that really rules our lives. You might have a plan that day, but you have to change it because everything depends on the wind direction, the velocity, the wave heights. Just because you've seen Isle Royale in the summer, you haven't really seen it. The lake is truly alive; it's got its moods, and there's no controlling it. We humans are generally trying to control everything, but the lake is out of our control."

The price for living in a place that seems to belong to another time is that the elements dictate nearly every major decision. And the elements can be whimsical. From the North Shore around to park headquarters on tiny Mott Island, boats must navigate Blake Point—what McDowell calls the crux move. "It's a headland and you can get strange currents; waves converge there and create real confused seas at times; the waves get squeezed. There are shoals all over— it can go from 400 feet deep to one foot deep in a matter of a hundred yards. You rely a lot on local knowledge, on ability to read and interpret charts, on electronics, radar, GPS, chart plotter, depth finder, Loran-C, compass. There's a reason there's ten major shipwrecks here. They were trained, skilled, licensed captains, but they ran aground."

With the Coast Guard hours away, Isle Royale's park rangers often have to fill in. "We sometimes have to go out and tow boats in to the nearest safe harbor," says McDowell. "We're asked to go out when other people are running back in."

But at the end of the day, even if it's a long one, rangers like Larry Kangas, Kyle McDowell, and Carl Terhaar feel the sacrifice is worth it. "I get to work in a place where other people take off a couple weeks from their jobs to come out and see," confides Terhaar. "They actually pay us to do this."

With a strenuous workout, warming rays, and the great outdoors, a canoeist enjoys the good life on Lake Richie, situated near the middle of Isle Royale National Park. The island's first visitors were hunter-gatherers who paddled here for copper, game, and berries thousands of years ago.

Northern Woodlands

Wave-sculpted sea caves, wild stretches of sandy beach, and dense groves of hemlocks and hardwoods make for many memorable outings at the APOSTLE ISLANDS NATIONAL SEASHORE. The 21 forested islands lying scattered off the tip of Wisconsin's Bayfield Peninsula in Lake Superior were not always so wild.

In the 1930s the national park service came here to assess the potential for a national park, but years of devastation by logging and other commercial activities made the islands unfit, says ranger Neil Houck. "Then 40 years later the area was established as a national lakeshore. Now 35 years after that the majority of the land base has been established as the nation's newest wilderness area."

A 22-year veteran of the park, Houck has a number of favorite places on the Apostle Islands. One is the north end of Outer Island, with its huge views of open water. "It gives you a real sense of being on the edge of the world." And the south end has one of the nicest beaches in the archipelago, offering "the feeling of being alone on a deserted island." Houck especially likes this place during spring and fall bird migrations, when thousands of birds flock through. In spring they funnel down the sandspit at the south end. "They'll come in clouds of hundreds," says Houck. "Hundreds of robins, hundreds of sparrows, warblers, thrushes. And the birds of prey follow them—the falcons and merlins that use Outer Island as a feeding station."

He also favors the sea caves found on some islands and along the mainland, where wave action over the millennia has eroded honeycombs into the 50-foot-high cliffs. In the winter ice from spray and spring water builds up in fanciful patterns and colors. "All the various colors of ice on a background of reddish sandstone with the frozen lake and blue sky make a pretty dramatic setting," enthuses Houck. On calm days he'll kayak back into the crevices, 200 feet or more, sometimes emerging from a different opening in the interconnected system.

One of the greatest trails in the park, according to Houck, is the Tombolo Trail on Stockton Island. The four-mile loop winds through a variety of environments. "You get to see a bog, dunes, the beach, and a pine forest, and all the diversity of animal life in these communities." The annual bird surveys on the Apostle Islands routinely count more species in this area than anywhere else in the park.

As for seasons, unlike Isle Royale the Apostle Islands National Seashore is open year round. If you can get there you can go, says Houck. A mere mile and a half separates the mainland from the nearest island. Part of the lake freezes by mid January. "I take my lead from the ice fishermen who are going out in snowmobiles and four-wheelers," says Houck. "I figure if the ice can hold them up, it can hold me up on skis."

On the east end of Lake Superior, the PICTURED ROCKS NATIONAL LAKESHORE, along the shores of Michigan's Upper Peninsula, preserves one of the most appealing stretches of Great Lakes coastline. Its 200-foot-high cliffs were hewn by wind, waves, and ice into terraces, arches, and knobs; minerals then colored them in red, orange, and rust. They extend over 12 of the park's 42-mile shoreline.

APOSTLE ISLANDS NATIONAL SEASHORE

For 17 years Ranger Greg Bruff has patrolled and explored these picturesque cliffs and beaches, though he says it seems like he arrived the day before yesterday. He likes to point out the lakeshore's unique ecology. "There's two or three plants here that are arctic disjuncts," he says. "They don't normally grow this far south, but because of the influence of Lake Superior they grow here." Thimbleberry and arctic crowberry are two such plants. Also fascinating to Bruff—and most visitors—are the Grand Sable Dunes. Rising and falling lake levels and weathering built up a tremendous wall of steeply pitched dunes that rises 300 feet above the lake and covers five square miles. Visitors climb the Sahara-like dunes for terrific views.

One of the best viewing places, says Bruff, is a place just west of the dunes called Log Slide. In the early 20th century loggers pushed their harvest down a wooden flume to the lake; the logs were gathered into a raft and floated over to Grand Marais for sawing. The view now encompasses dunes, sandy beach, the Au Sable Light Station, and the vast lake.

A good forested trail is the nine-mile Chapel Loop, which passes fantastically eroded rocks, a quiet beach, and high cliffs cut with deep recesses by wave action. North winds drive forceful six-foot waves against these cliffs. Bruff also likes the cliffside views at Miner's Castle, which take in the cliffs and, to the west, the national recreation area of Grand Island. From here there are trails to a sandy beach and back to 60-foot-high Miner's Falls. One thing Bruff appreciates about the Miner's Basin area is the long history. "We have old campsites there that go back 3,200 years," he says. With some of those campsites still in use, the area has indeed been well appreciated.

Sunset from Inspiration Point, a Bryce Canyon National Park classic, takes in the full glory of Bryce Amphitheater. The canyon's wilderness of hoodoos—phantom-like rock spires—was created by erosion of the

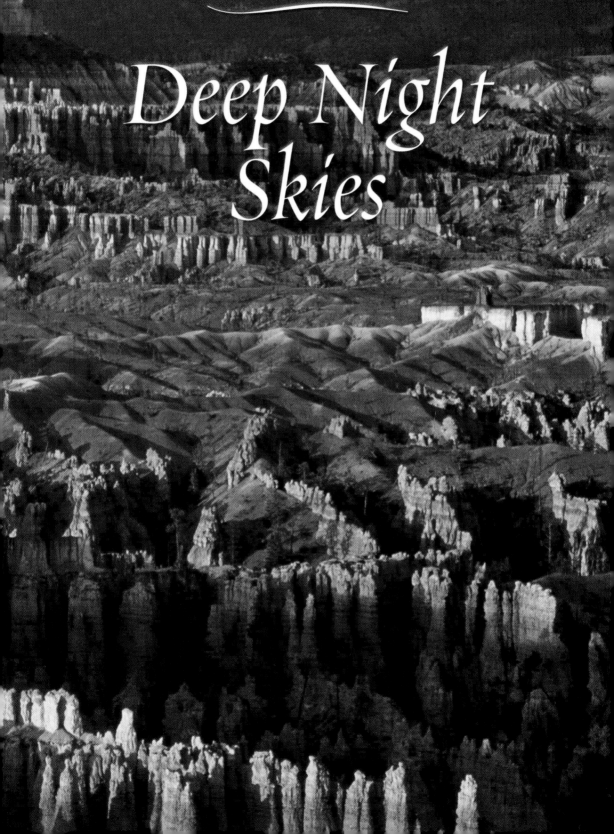

CHAPTER 4

Deep Night Skies

Stand just about anywhere on the edge of Bryce Canyon and you have the disorienting sense that you are staring into a vast ancient city of ruined stone temples and gigantic figurines. Angkor Wat comes to mind, or the clay warriors of Xian. After millions of years of erosion, the Paunsaugunt Plateau in southern Utah has opened into amphitheaters of fluted columns, spires, arches, bridges, and castles. The park's signature hoodoos—weirdly eroded spires—are past counting. In some places delicate, in others rugged, these rock formations take on rich hues of amber, salmon, and sienna, varying with the time of day and the season.

More than 1.5 million people a year come to Bryce to see the hoodoos and other natural sculpture. They drive at least some of the 17-mile road to Rainbow Point, stop at the overlooks, maybe hike a loop trail in Bryce Amphitheater near the visitor's center. That done, they're off to one of the area's bigger national parks, like Zion or the Grand Canyon—their real destination.

At only 56 square miles, Bryce Canyon is small for a national park in the West. "Bryce is more intimate than a place like Zion or the Grand Canyon," asserts chief ranger Brent McGinn. "Most foreign visitors will go to the Grand Canyon and not be able to grasp the immensity of it—it's outside their experience. Zion is intimidating because you're in the bottom of the canyon, and the walls are huge. But at Bryce you're on top of the plateau looking out at the long views and distances."

Having worked at Zion for seven years McGinn admits to keeping a soft spot in his heart for that park, but he loves Bryce for its immediacy. In the clear, crisp air—with rim elevations from 8,000 to 9,000 feet—badland formations such as Thor's Hammer and the Silent City seem close enough to reach out and touch. That's why, according to McGinn, Bryce has a disproportionate rescue work load. First of all, people are at a high elevation. It may not feel hot, but dehydration can become a big problem. Then, people start heading down into the canyon. Not until they start climbing out—sometimes a thousand feet or more over a few miles—do they realize how tough it is. "It only *appears* to be easier than Zion."

Like embrasures in a castle wall, "sky holes" pierce a fin of red rock along the Queens Garden Trail.
Such windows open up when frost and rain erode niches on both sides of the wall.

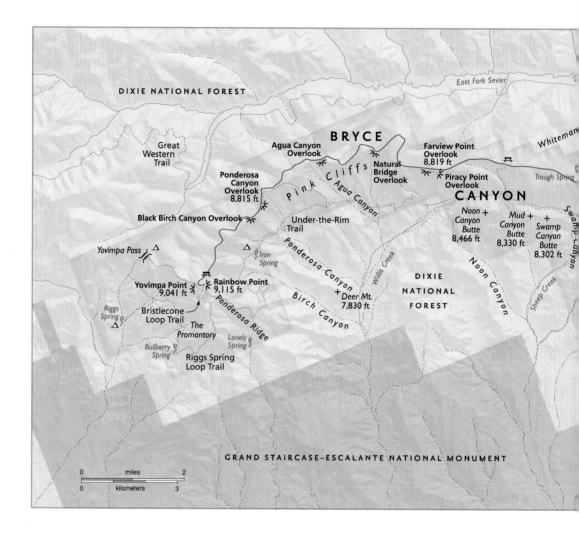

But once acclimated to the park's elevation and deceptive distances, people should stick around longer, believes McGinn. They tend to underestimate Bryce's potential for overnight stays. "The park is underutilized for backcountry camping," he says. Zion and Grand Canyon, on the other hand, often run out of backcountry permits. Unlike the day hikers, the overnighters are much more likely to see the mule deer, elk, pronghorns, and other things that may be a surprise at a park known mainly for its striking geology. "People try to come through and see Bryce in a day," says McGinn. "What they don't realize is that they're not seeing very much of it. We have 63 miles of trails, and they're beautiful."

He cites the Bristlecone Loop at the southern end of the park as one of his favorites. Its mix of tremendous vistas and ancient alpine forest is unique in the park. Twisted and stunted by harsh growing conditions, the remarkable bristlecone pine is one of the oldest living things on Earth, with a lifespan of around 5,000 years. Its resinous wood helps protect it from dessication, insects, and bacteria. The park further protects the bristlecones by not

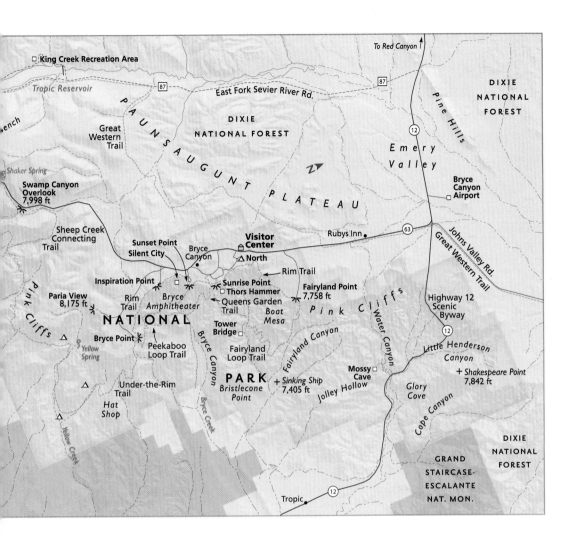

publishing the age and exact location of its older trees, though it does admit that the oldest is somewhere at Yovimpa Point on the Bristlecone Trail. At about 1,600 years, it is relatively young for a bristlecone. The "Methuselah" bristlecone, the world's oldest living tree at 4,765 years, grows in an undisclosed location in the White Mountains of southeastern California. An even older bristlecone—4,900 years old—was cut down in the Great Basin area of Nevada in 1964 by a researcher studying climate change.

As wonderful as they are, the trees go unnoticed by many people, but no one can miss the staggering views. A major thrill for McGinn is to share Bryce with newcomers. "I take them out to the rim, and I don't watch what they're looking at. I watch them. Even people who've worked in other parks are amazed at the the hundred-plus-mile views and the fact that in every part of that view there's something beautiful to look at, from the hoodoos that start almost right at your feet all the way out to Navajo Mountain on the other side of Lake Powell in Arizona. There aren't many places like that."

The hoodoos of Bryce have thousands of variations. Some look like giant drip castles or stalagmites, others like modern sculpture or bizarre creatures from another planet. It's easy to see why the Paiutes considered them men turned to stone by wrathful gods. They called the local badlands *Unka-timpe-wa-wince-pock-ich* (red rocks standing like men in a bowl-shaped recess). Less cumbersome are other Paiute names clinging to area features: *Paunsaugunt* (home of the beaver), the town of *Panguitch,* (big fish), and the plateau from which the Grand Canyon is carved—*Kaibab* (mountain lying down).

Hoodoos are found in many places, but the term originated here—possibly a variant of "voodoo" or the Paiute term for the formation. Because the region's first white settlers included Mormons well versed in ancient Hebrew, there is speculation that Mormons may have coined the odd term from a similar-sounding Hebrew word for "aboriginal person." The fatter sandstone hoodoos of Goblin Valley to the northeast are snubbed by Bryce lovers as "couch-potato hoodoos." Not far southeast, Kodachrome Basin looks like a miniature Bryce, but its spires were created by geysers that clogged with sediment. In short, then, Bryce is the king of hoodoos, and its hoodoos stand as foreground decoration for wide-angled views that never fail to uplift the spirit.

Along with those impossibly long views come an immense silence and a night sky that is the envy of the national park system. "I gotta admit," says McGinn, "when I started out in the park service I was more about grizzly bears and elk and big things like that. I didn't realize until I started reading some of the history of the parks why they were established. Somewhere in between the 1930s and now, a lot of us have lost that sense that they were established as a refuge from the masses, as a place where it was quiet and where you had those views of the night sky away from city lights and the hustle and bustle. Visitors don't usually come here for that, but it really hits them—the natural quiet, the unpolluted views. It made me step back a little bit and think."

Bryce is serious about its night skies. Though not the hot political issue that, say, wetlands protection is at Everglades National Park, the night skies movement has developed to the point that the park service has a full-time program, currently headquartered at Bryce. When a 1999 study found that two-thirds of 189 parks were reporting light pollution, the Night Sky Team was born. They work with local communities to improve lighting that is often inefficient, directed pointlessly into the air instead of toward the ground. As ranger Mark Biel points out, "We try to show communities there's a benefit if they spend money to improve night skies. More people will want to come here." Air pollution from Las Vegas and other places can also affect night sky clarity, as well as visibility during the daytime.

When asked how Bryce gets the title of number-one night sky in the national park sys-

Snow adds sparkling contrast to formations in Agua Canyon, visible in the southern part of the park.
The park service used to name prominent hoodoos—"Hunter," "Rabbit," "Backpacker," and so on—but
has dropped the practice since erosion changes the shapes of formations over the decades.

TOURS WITH RANGERS

Early morning light brings out subtle hues in a monumental hoodoo along the Queens Garden Trail.
Hoodoos form with differential erosion along ridgetops, first splitting apart from each other and then
weathering into their own weird shapes.

Bristlecone pines cling to a rocky perch beneath towering hoodoos on the Queens Garden Trail, while a hiker checks out distant formations. The efficient use of sparse resources makes bristlecone pines among the oldest living organisms on earth, capable of surviving for 5,000 years.

Following pages: Trail riders near Sunrise Point head down into Bryce Canyon on a two-hour trek to the canyon floor and back. Bryce was first surveyed in 1872 by one-armed Maj. J. W. Powell and geographer Almon Thompson; intrepid automobile travelers arrived by 1915, and the park was established in 1928.

tem, McGinn responds, "You're talking to the chief ranger at Bryce, and I've just decided that it is." Actually, there's a bit more to the story. The night sky team made a trip several years ago and determined that Bryce at that time had the darkest night sky. "It wasn't a statistically valid survey," confesses McGinn, "especially when Zion happened to be cloudy that night." But with Zion a bit closer to a little more light pollution—45 miles from the town of St. George—it's doubtful Zion could have matched Bryce for starry brilliance. "I was at Zion when they did the survey," McGinn recalls, "and I was highly upset. But now that I'm at Bryce I think it's a great idea. I don't want them to do the survey again."

Suffice it to say that Bryce Canyon ranks as one of the darkest areas in the lower 48 states and has become a mecca for stargazers. The skies are so primitively dark at night that Venus can cast shadows. At star parties throughout the year, amateur astronomers set up telescopes, compare notes, and happily explain the workings of the heavens to visitors. During full moons, when the light is too bright for stargazing, rangers lead hikes among the hoodoos, the moonlight blazing down into the canyon.

The chief of resource management and research, Kristin Legg has worked at Bryce Canyon for two years. When she wants to get away from it all, she gets up early in the morning when the light is just beginning to tap the top notes of the canyon formations. With the sun sliding in among the russet and crimson hoodoos, she heads out on one of the park's longer hikes. The eight-mile Fairyland Loop, for instance, is nice because it starts out on the rim, then heads down into the hoodoos. At the south end of the park, the equally challenging Riggs Spring Loop is another of Legg's favorites: "It's a little more remote backcountry, more forested, but you still get to look up along the rim. Getting up early to go for a hike or a ski and being out there by myself or with just a few people and experiencing the park in that way is pretty incredible." As for seasons, "in the wintertime when it snows and the light is on the hoodoos—it's amazing. The air is crisp and cool, so the light is more vibrant and there's more contrast. Towards summer you have lingering daylight and a softer light."

One of the projects Legg is currently working on at Bryce is "sound management" or "soundscape monitoring." In addition to its night skies, Bryce is noted for its quietness, a quality more and more valued in a noisy world. Acoustic studies have showed that the natural silence of Bryce is often equivalent to that of a recording studio. Yet helicopter and airplane tours, as well as other extraneous noise, sometimes interfere with the pristine quiet. "Vehicles, even our own, are a main source of noise pollution right now, as well as scenic overflights," says Legg. "We'll be working with commercial users to see what's feasible to do."

Still another project involves returning natural fires to the ecosystem. "We're going to be doing not only prescribed fires and suppression but also wildland fire use. If there's a lightning strike and the weather and other conditions are appropriate we'll allow that fire to burn. It's going to be exciting to see how things change in the park."

Another ranger, Kristen Meyer, is a full-time fire technician. She works with the local community, including the little town of Tropic, to address concerns about wild and prescribed fires. "I've noticed a bit more acceptance over the years," she says. Right now about half the people understand the ecological value of fires, while the other half have concerns. The park's position is that fires clear out underbrush that could later cause out-of-control fires; they return nutrients to the soil; and they keep plant communities in balance. A great deal of study goes into a burn. "You have a burn plan and burn boss," explains Meyer. "And then there's firefighters and other contingency resources nearby just in case." To assess what needs to be burned when, Meyer monitors the forest conditions and climatology of a particular area throughout the season. She and her team use roads and meadows as boundaries, though sometimes they can put out the edges as they move along. They generally ignite the fires with drip torches that employ a mixture of diesel and gasoline. Sometimes they use helicopters to drop little ping-pong-size balls filled with a chemical that combusts shortly after they hit the ground.

Saddles hang ready for the next rider at Canyon Trail Rides, which leads horseback and mule riding trips into Bryce Canyon. With the horse doing the walking, visitors are free to observe the amazing scenery, rather than their footing.

TOURS WITH RANGERS

As a fire ecologist, Meyer knows her trees. Hence one of her favorite hiking trails in the park is the Riggs Spring Loop. "I don't see many people on that trail," she says, "and I like the large spruce trees at the higher elevations of the trail." The forest and the long unblemished views on the trail make it spectacular. "I grew up on the Front Range [of Colorado] where there's so much encroachment and development going on, but here you look outward and you realize you are surrounded completely by nature. There's so much public land around here."

Ranger Jennifer Heroux is similarly impressed with the amount of public land surrounding Bryce Canyon National Park. Just west of the park lies the impressive Red Canyon, within Dixie National Forest; the canyon's colors are brilliant reds and greens created by the iron oxides in the rocks and the large ponderosa pines. And heading eastward "you go through some of the most spectacular scenery in southern Utah," maintains Heroux. "The road skirts the top of the Grand Staircase-Escalante National Monument, and the scenery between the town of Escalante and the town of Boulder is phenomenal."

The tremendous national monument takes in 1.7 million acres of white cliffs, banded mesas, and sandstone canyons in the high desert. The Grand Staircase refers to the series of huge tilted cliffs stepping south to the Grand Canyon and walking through 200 million years of geological history. Named for their rock colors, the stairsteps of pink, gray, white, vermilion, and chocolate correspond to different geological periods. The highest rock layers of Bryce are the most recent, those at the bottom of the Grand Canyon the oldest at 1.5 billion years. Down in the depths of Bryce Canyon, the Dakota Formation rocks are more than 350 million years old.

After graduating from Hampshire College in Massachusetts, with studies in literature and photography, Heroux did a two-year stint with AmeriCorps, a domestic Peace Corps, before finding a job with the park service. Since 2001 she has worked at Everglades, Yellowstone, and Canyonlands. She fell in love with Bryce Canyon on her first visit here, hiking in the main amphitheater. "Around every bend was a new color, a new shape, and a new awakening in my imagination. I've never seen anything like it, and I've been around the globe. There's nothing quite like it in the world as far as the rock formations. Cedar Breaks and Red Canyon are in close proximity and are also part of the Claron Formation. They're very beautiful, but nothing like Bryce Canyon."

The key difference is in the rocks themselves. "Unlike most of the rock that you see throughout northern Arizona and southern Utah, it is not sandstone. It's limestone, which is much more soluble. The rock, being softer, can respond to the types of weather and erosion that we have going on to create these beautiful formations. With the multitude of cold nights, any moisture trapped inside the rock will freeze and expand, and slowly but surely over time it begins to sculpt out those hoodoos. There's also regular erosion from storms and snowmelt, but we don't have any active streams or rivers. So the cold nights and the

White aspen trunks stand out against evergreens, growing here along the canyon rim at about 8,500 feet elevation. Aspens often grow in the sunny, damp areas between forests and meadows, their summer green and autumn gold foliage adding shimmering, scented overtones to the hillsides.

summer thunderstorms are the elements that you can see shaping the canyon today." The freeze-thaw cycle occurs up to 200 times a year; that process combined with other weathering slices away at the rim at the rate of about one foot every 50 years.

A typical day for Heroux in her role as interpretive ranger at Bryce involves three main duties. About a third of her day is spent doing ranger talks and walks and other programs; another third she spends at the visitor center fielding questions; and with the rest of her day she preps herself by going out and learning more about the park—taking hikes by herself, studying, and talking with researchers in the field.

A perfect day for Heroux would begin at sunrise at any of the rim's viewpoints, since they almost all face eastward. Most visitors unfortunately miss this quintessential time of day at Bryce, she says. She would then hike the Queens Garden and Peekaboo Loop trails, a combined walk of four to five hours. Or one of the undertraveled trails, such as the trail to Tower Bridge, starting at Sunrise Point. "Not many people do it because it's more strenuous. It's just a three-mile hike but it has an elevation change of over 800 feet, and Tower Bridge is a fantastic feature in the park." One of the more unusual formations, Tower Bridge is a narrow rock bridge running between two tremendous monoliths of stone. Heroux's ideal day would end at sunset out at Rainbow and Yovimpa Points, at the far southern end of the park.

For law enforcement ranger Brenda Bentley, a typical day is far different from Heroux's. "My major in college was wildlife biology and my minor just for fun was criminal justice," she says. "I had no idea what I wanted to do, but when I went to Yellowstone I realized they actually go really well together. I was working in the backcountry and I loved it—I was out hiking the trails every day. But it was frustrating to see people who would approach wildlife or leave trash all over their campsites. I could tell them what to do, but I couldn't enforce anything. That's why I got into law enforcement."

Bentley has a sweet voice that belies her no-nonsense attitude. "Now even if I'm just educating people, they listen a little better to somebody who has a gun on their hip. If you don't, they sometimes say things like, 'Who are you to tell me what to do?' Little do they know that we're also carrying radios and have friends who carry guns."

The most common infraction at Bryce is speeding. "We have deer that get hit all the time. We also have the threatened Utah prairie dog here, and quite a few get hit." Drugs and alcohol are not much of a problem at Bryce—lying more out of the way than many parks, it tends to attract mostly families and serious nature lovers. More common is the throwing of cigarette

TOURS WITH RANGERS

Waxy-leaved, red-stemmed manzanita (opposite) splashes color throughout the park; the word means "little apple" in Spanish. An endangered white-tailed prairie dog (above) stands on alert; circling birds of prey elicit an urgent series of quick yaps, followed by disappearance into burrows.

Following pages: Thor's Hammer and other oddly eroded rocks cast early morning shadows in Bryce Amphitheater. Once upon a time, animal-like creatures lived here; they changed themselves to people but were so wicked that Coyote turned them to stone. So claims a Paiute legend.

butts out the window, for which Brenda will happily write out a 50-dollar ticket. Some visitors, especially from other countries, are surprised to be pulled over for such habitual littering.

In a normal summer week, Bentley will respond to four or five emergency calls, working with rescue squads to evacuate accident victims. "People go down into the canyon without proper footwear. They sprain their ankle, break their ankle, break the lower part of their leg. We also have a lot of visitors who aren't used to elevations; they start hiking and get altitude sickness. And we get quite a few cardiac calls. Down in the canyon their cell phones don't work, so another visitor will see them and report it to us."

When she's off duty, Bentley likes hiking along the 23-mile Under-the-Rim Trail, which takes in a mind-boggling array of geological wonders, including the multicolored striations of Claron limestone, hidden springs dashed with wildflowers, and the memorable Pink Cliffs. In the erosional fantasy world of the Hat Shop, hikers can well appreciate the assessment of pioneer rancher Ebenezer Bryce, for whom the canyon was named: "It's a hell of a place to lose a cow." Near the southern end of the park, the hike climbs sharply to 9,100 feet and provides awe-inspiring views of badlands and mesas for a hundred miles or more. Bentley is particularly impressed with the park's ample bird life. The Under-the-Rim Trail offers her a chance to see, among others, Cooper's hawks, northern flickers, violet-green swallows, Steller's jays, pygmy nuthatches, vesper sparrows, and broad-tailed hummingbirds. She has also seen ospreys, large flocks of turkeys, peregrines that nest on cliff edges, and condors—endangered raptors with wingspans of up to 9.5 feet—that occasionally soar over the park, looking for prey. Condors have recently begun roosting on Lava Point over at Zion National Park.

Whether it's working with people, the law, fire, sound management, or any of the other daily challenges of Bryce Canyon National Park, rangers Bentley, Heroux, Meyer, and the others seem particularly suited to their jobs. Says Kristin Legg: "I like thinking about how we can make the park a better place for the people that come here. I spend a lot of time behind the computer, but it's an amazing opportunity to work at Bryce, and I think I'm a very lucky person to get to live here and have this job." She cites a survey showing that 95 percent of visitors last year gave their Bryce experience a thumbs up. "Many visitors are just awestruck." You could say the same for the rangers who work here, who enrich themselves and others with long timeless views framed by hoodoos and ancient pines. And the views never seem to get old—probably because it took so long to get the scenery just right. Job satisfaction is high in a park that was 350 million years in the making.

A deep azure sky silhouettes a spindly bristlecone pine, which appears to brush the clouds above the canyon rim. Noted for its ultra-clear skies, Bryce Canyon National Park has become a major destination for astronomy enthusiasts, as well as those who simply like their views unfiltered by pollution.

Canyon Country

Ranger Tom Haridan, a park service employee since 1972, is used to fielding calls from magazine editors wanting to know the "secret" places of ZION NATIONAL PARK in southwestern Utah. Without hesitation he whispers slyly, "It's Zion Canyon." That's the non-secret secret, the reason everybody comes here—for the canyon itself. "When the park was created it was very small, but it was centered right around this canyon."

Haridan elaborates. "If I had a favorite spot in the park, it wouldn't be some far-off hard-to-get-to place; it would just be one of these nice classic hikes in the park like Angels Landing, but maybe at a time of day or year when there weren't so many other people." He uses words like "invigorating" and "grueling" to describe the hike, which ascends 1,400 feet in 2.5 miles, as one of the best in the entire national park system over a route that probably would not be chosen nowadays. "There's a part that's as wide as your desk, and it drops off 200 feet on one side and 900 feet on the other. It's not for people who are afraid of heights."

Haridan says the hikes in Zion tend to be "all or nothing—easy or strenuous." Those

ZION NATIONAL PARK

that stay along the canyon bottom are generally easy, like the "marvelous" Riverside Walk, a stroll along the Virgin River through a narrow canyon of sheer sandstone cliffs. It passes through bird-filled stands of cottonwood and ash and by hanging gardens of maidenhair fern and golden columbine. The walk ends at The Narrows, a defile with walls 2,000 feet high and in places a mere 18 feet apart.

Instead of listing hidden places, Haridan prefers to talk about capturing a mood, or an essence. He says that people who check out the photographs on the Zion website suspect that the color has been enhanced. Not true, he promises. "Six percent humidity is not uncommon, so the sky's as blue as blue can be. And when you have the brilliant sun shining on these red canyon walls, and you're looking up through deep green cottonwood trees—that's the kind of secret we try to tell people about."

Haridan routinely encourages people to slow down, not race from one national park to the next. "The secret to enjoying this place is just taking the time to do it. You can go for a walk, or just sit on a rock."

Another southern Utah canyon park, CAPITOL REEF NATIONAL PARK embraces the parallel ridges of the Waterpocket Fold, an uplift eroded into a wonderland of huge domes, labyrinthine canyons, slickrock cliffs, and water-filled sandstone depressions. Geologists call the fold a monocline, and consider Capitol Reef one of the biggest and best exposed on the continent. Capitol Reef takes its name from an especially colorful section of the fold near the Fremont River, where sheer cliffs formed a barrier to travel for early pioneers and reminded them of an ocean reef.

CAPITOL REEF NATIONAL PARK

"What I like about Capitol Reef is the diversity," says ranger Riley Mitchell. "There's a federally designated rural historic landscape, a free-flowing river, and of course the geology." The three-square-mile historic area encompasses the old community of Fruita and the largest orchard system in the National Park Service. In contrast to the towering rock walls, Fruita is a green oasis created by Mormons in the late 1800s on fields that were abandoned by Fremont Indians 600 years earlier. Old irrigation ditches still water apple, apricot, and peach trees—whose fruit may be picked by anyone—and mule deer graze on orchard grasses and alfalfa.

As for the rest of the landscape, "I tell people it's geology in your face," says Mitchell. "It's like dissecting a frog is to a biologist. It's just right there and you can't escape it." She likes the easy two-mile roundtrip hike to Hickman Bridge. "You walk along the river for a while, you get a little bit of upper Great Basin vegetation as you climb out of the basin, there's some canyon desert walking, and the spectacle is the 135-foot natural rock bridge. There's a lot of bang for the buck."

Though there are plenty of slot canyons and other amazing features that are remote and difficult to access, Capitol Reef has a wealth of views and hikes of varying degrees of difficulty within handy reach. "The thing about Capitol Reef that's so special," says Mitchell, "is that it's sort of a microcosm of the entire Colorado Plateau, on an intimate scale. It's nice to be able to get into a canyon like Grand Wash and see up close and personal the effects of erosion."

Night falls on the curled tip of Cape Cod, where the Wood End Light flashes its signal out across Cape Cod Bay every ten seconds. Dating from 1896, the square lighthouse was the center of a busy fishing community during the turn of the 20th century. The marshy area is now quiet year round despite the proximity of Provincetown.

CHAPTER 5

The Calm of the Cape

R anger Sue Moynihan tells a story about a defining moment for her at Cape Cod National Seashore. She moved here from Great Smoky Mountains National Park in North Carolina in August 1998. "We came at the height of the season," she says. "My husband had grown up here so he knew what to expect. I remember we were sitting at a restaurant eating lunch. I was having trouble finding child care, we were dealing with August traffic and all the logistics of relocating, and I said to my husband, 'I think we've made a terrible mistake. I think we should go back to the Smokies.' We'd been here for four days, and I hadn't had the time to drive out to my duty station. So one evening we got in the car and drove out to Province Lands. And when we dropped over the hill at Pilgrim Lake, I saw the dunes for the first time. The calming effect was unbelievable, and I said, 'It's okay. We can stay.'"

Ask anyone who lives and works on this legendary Massachusetts peninsula what makes it unique in the national park system and that person will tell you about its tight blend of natural and human history. From the Indians and Pilgrims, to the whalers and lighthouse keepers, to the artists and beachcombers, Cape Cod has welcomed a steady progress of people. But despite that progress, the Cape, thanks largely to the national seashore, still holds miles and miles of unblemished coastal landscape.

For an example of the ongoing mix of cultural and natural history, Moynihan points to Old Harbor Life-Saving Station at Race Point Beach. It stands as a reminder of the power of the sea to influence people's lives. "There's a strong life-saving history on Cape Cod," she says. "On Thursday nights during the summer the staff present a reenactment of a 1902 rescue drill at Old Harbor. You're transported back in time, because the staff are wearing surf-whites, the keeper's in a uniform, and they fire the line out of the Lyle gun out to a simulated shipwreck just as they would have in 1902. What's wonderful is that the public gets to take

Boat and gear look ready for action at the Old Harbor Life-Saving Museum. Before World War II and the arrival of better weather prediction and navigation instruments, 13 lifesaving stations operated on the Cape.

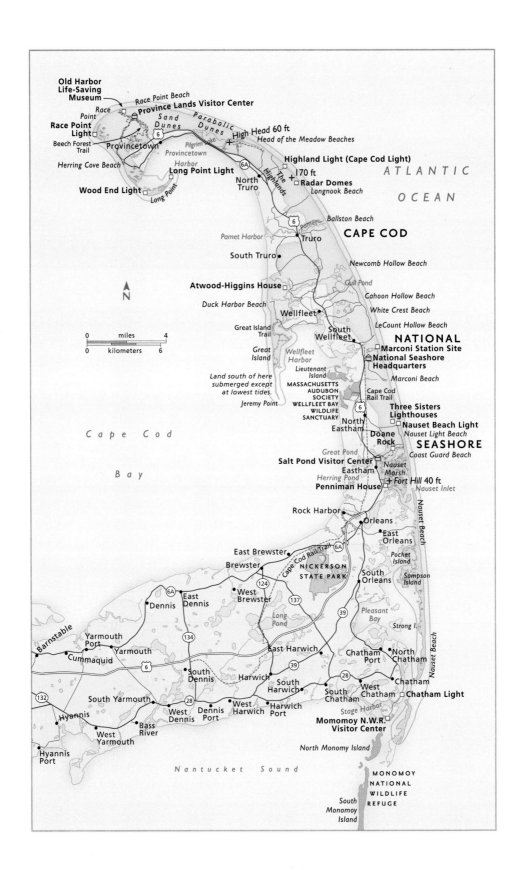

Old Harbor
Life-Saving
Museum
Race Point Beach
Race Point
Province Lands Visitor Center
Race
Point
Race Point
Light
Sand
Dunes
Parabolic
Dunes
High Head 60 ft
Head of the Meadow Beaches
Beech Forest
Trail
Provincetown
Pilgrim
Lake
Provincetown
Highland Light (Cape Cod Light)
Herring Cove Beach
Harbor
Long Point Light
North
Truro
170 ft
Radar Domes
Longnook Beach
Wood End Light
Long Point
ATLANTIC
OCEAN

CAPE COD

The Highlands
Ballston Beach
Pamet
6
Pamet Harbor
Truro
Newcomb Hollow Beach
South Truro
Gull Pond
Atwood-Higgins House
Cahoon Hollow Beach
Duck Harbor Beach
Wellfleet
White Crest Beach
Great Island
Trail
South
Wellfleet
LeCount Hollow Beach
Great
Island
Wellfleet
Harbor
NATIONAL
Marconi Station Site
National Seashore
Headquarters
Land south of here
submerged except
at lowest tides.
Lieutenant
Island
MASSACHUSETTS
AUDUBON
SOCIETY
WELLFLEET BAY
WILDLIFE
SANCTUARY
Marconi Beach
Jeremy Point
Cape Cod
Rail Trail
6
North
Eastham
Three Sisters
Lighthouses
Nauset Beach Light
Nauset Light Beach
Doane
Rock
SEASHORE
Coast Guard Beach

Cape Cod

Bay

Great Pond
Salt Pond Visitor Center
Eastham
Penniman House
Nauset
Marsh
Fort Hill 40 ft
Herring Pond
Nauset Inlet
Rock Harbor
Orleans
East
Orleans
East Brewster
Cape Cod Rail Trail
6A
Pochet
Island
Brewster
NICKERSON
STATE PARK
South
Orleans
Sampson
Island
6A
East
Dennis
124
West
Brewster
137
Pleasant
Bay
Strong I.
Dennis
Long
Pond
39
Barnstable
134
Yarmouth
Port
East Harwich
Chatham
Port
North
Chatham
Cummaquid
Yarmouth
6
39
28
West
Chatham
Chatham
South
Dennis
Harwich
South
Harwich
South
Chatham
Chatham Light
132
South Yarmouth
28
West
Dennis
Dennis
Port
West
Harwich
Harwich
Port
Stage Harbor
Momomoy N.W.R.
Visitor Center
Hyannis
Bass
River
West
Yarmouth
North Monomy Island
Hyannis
Port
Nantucket Sound
MONOMOY
NATIONAL
WILDLIFE
REFUGE
South
Monomoy
Island

0   miles   4
0   kilometers   6

N

Captain Edward Penniman built his French Second Empire-style house in Eastham in 1868. Many area sea captains, rich from whaling and the China trade, erected lavish homes as emblems of their success.

part. Likewise, in 1902 when the surfmen were doing this drill, the community would come out and watch and participate."

Park historian Bill Burke has been here, serving in various capacities, since 1988. He observes that Cape Cod was one of the first units of the national park system created as an overlay on existing towns and private lands. "Most units are created out of big chunks of federally owned wilderness, or big donations from Rockefeller," he says. "Here there were significant pockets of undeveloped land, but they were all intertwined with the six outer Cape towns. It's an interesting blend of the human imprint that makes it more than just a wildlife refuge. It's a very complex mosaic."

One of Burke's jobs is to work with the local communities to see that their pre-park way of life remains intact. The continuity—of traditional boatmaking, shellfishing, berrypicking, and other things that set Cape Cod apart—is an important part of his mission. "It's not just about opening the beach in June and managing endangered piping plovers and water quality," he asserts. "It's about the park being aware of and trying to work with the six towns on every aspect of how this place looks and functions for year-rounders as well as for visitors."

One of Burke's current projects is a fascinating study of the people who live in the dune shacks outside Provincetown and Truro. Tennessee Williams, Jack Kerouac, Eugene O'Neill, and many other writers and artists have stayed in the cottages since they were built in the 1920s and '30s. Many of the current owners are descendants of the original builders, who were never able to get title to the land underneath their cottages. Thus a complex social-legal issue has arisen around who will own the cottages when the leases expire in the next decade or so. "We're undertaking an ethnographic study of those people," says Burke. "much like an ethnographer would go into a tribe in Africa. We're looking at those families, their backgrounds, what their family networks are, their kinship webs, to determine whether those families can stay. It's very subjective and very emotional for all parties involved."

Most of such formally recognized traditional cultural properties (TCPs) have been Native American communities and sacred sites. Burke admits that this group is very different from the traditional notion of a native community more often found in the western states. "There's nothing cohesive on the surface," he says. "The people are by their own admission primarily loners, and they're out there for solitude. It's a spectacular dune landscape, and there's only 18 cottages spread over thousands of acres." A few of the cottages have, in fact, already reverted back to the park and are being used for artist-in-residence programs through local arts organizations. So one way or another, the tradition of artistic creation by the seaside will continue on Cape Cod.

All in all, Burke says, Cape Cod National Seashore holds about 75 historic buildings, from the 1730 Atwood-Higgins House—a traditional Cape Cod bungalow with gray shingle siding, high windows, and big central chimney—to lesser known mid-20th-century houses designed by the likes of Marcel Breuer and other transplanted Bauhaus architects who had fled the Nazis in the 1930s. There are also a number of picturesque 19th-century lighthouses, and a Cold War radar station that, says Burke, was the first line of defense against Soviet bombers flying across the Atlantic.

In addition to its many cultural assets, Cape Cod National Seashore is, naturally, home to a wide variety of coastal flora and fauna. Plant ecologist Stephen Smith works behind the scenes to evaluate changes in the park's different ecosystems and to try to determine which changes are man-made and which are natural. He is especially intrigued by Cape Cod's freshwater wetlands. "A lot of people don't even know about them," he says, "and they're some of the most beautiful and unique habitats on the Cape."

Among the various wetlands, the vernal ponds, which form in the spring and dry up later in the year, are an important breeding habitat for a number of amphibian species, including the spotted salamander, Fowler's toad, and spadefoot toad. Smith recently completed a two-year study of some 350 interdunal wetlands in the

Emerald-toned wetlands grace the interior of Cape Cod National Seashore, visible here off the Beech Forest Trail in the Province Lands area. The one-mile trail skirts a shallow pond, as well as dunes encroaching upon the forest.

TOURS WITH RANGERS

The extensive parabolic dunes area in the north part of Cape Cod began forming about 6,000 years ago as currents carried sand northward; wind then sculpted the dunes and beach grass stabilized them. The area now measures about five miles long and one mile wide, with dunes rising 40 to 100 feet high.

Sifting the sea: At Salt Pond, ranger Phil Kyle and eager students net shrimp, hermit crabs, clams, and other marine life. Dikes and causeways built in the 19th and early 20th centuries restricted tide flow crucial to life in the coastal marshes; the national seashore has embarked on a program of estuarine restoration.

Following pages: On a field trip to Cape Cod National Seashore, schoolchildren from Roxbury, Vermont, use Coast Guard Beach for a classroom—and a kitchen. A lesson here could cover anything from coastal geology and marine ecology to early American history and environmental literature.

parabolic dunes area in the north part of the Cape. "It's a vast expanse of sand dunes that looks much like a desert environment until you really get in there and see that between the dunes these vernal wetlands occur, and you've got little oases of plant and animal communities." Among the plants are insectivorous sundews that catch insects on sticky threads, and orchids that bloom in summer, spreading a red and pink carpet over the wetlands.

The Cape also holds numerous kettle ponds—big round ponds that formed during the last ice age when debris from glacial runoff created Cape Cod. "The glaciers left these big blocks of ice which made depressions in the landscape. They melted, and since they intersect with the groundwater table they're permanent freshwater ponds. Some of the kettle ponds are amazingly oligotrophic, which

TOURS WITH RANGERS

means nutrient poor, which translates into incredibly clear water. As a result in some ponds in the early spring you have up to 40 feet visibility, which you don't have in many places in the world nowadays."

Another park scientist, Mark Adams has logged many hours studying the Cape's long past. As a geographer and cartographer he has teamed up with a geologist from the nearby Woods Hole Oceanographic Institute to examine how the Cape has changed over the years and centuries. They are looking at shoreline measurements taken as long ago as the 1890s, then comparing them with more recent aerial photographs and satellite images and discovering some interesting things about the Cape.

"At the time of the last ice age," explains Adams, "Georges Bank, which is a big fishing ground north of us, would dissipate the wave energy." But with sea level rising since the ice age, Georges Bank has become submerged, so the Cape has become exposed to a lot more wave energy from the North Atlantic. "The Cape wants to orient itself perpendicular to the wave energy. So as we get more unimpeded wave energy, we're guessing the whole Cape is going to want to rotate to the north. Sand's piling up in Provincetown at the north end of the spit rather rapidly, and in the center of the Cape it's eroding really quickly. In a given year up to ten feet of the cliff will just drop away. The average is three to six feet per year, which is quite a lot, particularly if you live next to it."

During a typical week, Adams might spend three days in his office analyzing data. The rest of the time he'll be out surveying on the beach, mentoring in the high school, or hacking through the shrubs, working with a wildlife biologist or ranger to locate boundaries. Sometimes he'll strap a GPS unit to the handlebars of a bicycle and try to map some of the unplanned—and unwanted—mountain bike trails that people cut through the woods. "My work life and home life blend in a way, because I spend a lot of time on the beaches, both mapping and marking changes and then looking at the waves for surfing."

He lives in a rented farmhouse in the middle of the Cape, which he considers one of his favorite areas of the park. He likes kayaking down the Pamet River near his house, then climbing over the dunes to Ballston Beach. Often he'll jog the little valleys that progress from pine forest to coastal brush to beach grass and then out onto the beach. "It's this sequence where you get more and more sky as you go through, and you can smell the ocean and feel the temperature change and the humidity. It all opens up at the beach." And Ballston is one of the less crowded beaches.

"People think of Cape Cod as sort of an urban park," says Adams, "because it's close to a lot of urban centers—two hours from Boston and Providence. But there's so many places that have a wildness about them, where you only have to walk a few steps sometimes to get completely away from the crowds."

At Coast Guard Beach, a wet-suited surfer waxes his board for a non-slippery ride. Below, a male fiddler crab displays his enlarged claw. The crabs emerge from their mudflat burrows at low tide to feed and defend territory; a claw lost during battle will grow back.

Interpretive ranger Tom Parsons has a similar outlook: "The vast majority of people who come here go to the beaches, and you can pretty easily get away from that if you're willing to explore, to go off paved routes and marked trails."

His idea of a great day on the Cape? "For something different, I like to go on unmapped hikes out into the dunes." Following old roads, old trails, or animal trails, he heads off with a compass, or sometimes just uses the Provincetown Monument, a giant granite tower, as a guide. "You start wandering and you come across coyotes and blueberries and Juneberries and cranberry bogs, all these hidden forests. You can't really get too lost before you find either the ocean or the bay or Route 6."

Parsons revels in the spontaneous episode, the serendipitous find. Like the most productive blueberry bush he'd ever seen—more blue than green—out in the dunes. Or the time he took two teenage brothers out on a canoe trip. The brothers grew bored and began quarreling. Then, as if Parsons had called it down, an osprey dove right in front of them and caught a fish. "They were so in awe—it was the best child-calming drug ever. They turned right around and became quiet and really into it." In fact, watching these minor miracles of people interacting with nature is the most exciting part of his job. "We know we've done our jobs when people ask good questions and they're thanking us repeatedly for bringing them out to those areas. That's rewarding."

Paradoxically for someone who likes wandering off the beaten path, Parsons's favorite viewpoint in the park is from the Province Lands Visitor Center. The observation deck stands about only a hundred feet high, but with everything else at sea level it's the highest thing around. "You get a breathtaking panoramic view of the Province Lands, which is a pine-oak forest with dunes mixed in, and you can see the ocean and across Cape Cod Bay over to Plymouth on a clear day. On a really clear day you can see the top halves of the buildings in Boston." With Boston more than 50 miles away, the view is indeed breathtaking.

Naturalist and ranger Jenna Sammartino came to Cape Cod nine years ago, fell in love with it, and has never left. As a seasonal ranger she has worked a wide variety of jobs, including freelance writing, to make ends meet in the lean season. That is, she says, simply the way of life for year-round Cape Codders. She has an infectious enthusiasm for the Cape's tradition of literary naturalists and for its seamless mix of cultural and natural history.

One of Sammartino's favorite places to take visitors is Coast Guard Beach. "That's the start of the Great Beach," she says, "a term coined by Henry David Thoreau in his book *Cape Cod.*" At about 30 miles, it's the longest unbroken, undeveloped sandy stretch on the east coast. "I love that area in particular because things that take hundreds of thousands of years to happen elsewhere, geologically speaking, liter-

TOURS WITH RANGERS

An early morning fisherman casts for striped bass at Race Point, on the Cape's northern end. Since prehistoric times people have been hauling in Cape Cod's abundant seafood. And as in those days, no license is required for saltwater fishing—just a long rod and a little luck.

ally happen in a span of decades out here." The way the beaches continue to exist is by rolling over themselves toward the mainland. When the ocean hammers the beach, it transfers that sand to the marsh side and the dunes can build up again.

Sammartino speaks lovingly of another Cape Cod classic, *The Outermost House*. In the 1920s writer Henry Beston built a beach shack—known locally as a camp—at Coast Guard Beach and spent a year chronicling the cycles of nature at the shoreline. The book, says Sammartino, "could make an Iowa farmer ache for the ocean." In 1978 a massive winter blizzard swept his house, by then something of a landmark, out to sea. "It doesn't really matter that the house is not there anymore," Sammartino says. "You can still walk down that beach and feel what he felt and smell what he smelled and see what he saw."

Coast Guard Beach is more famous now as a consistent placer in the Top Ten Beaches in the country, an annual survey conducted by Dr. Stephen Leatherman, director of the Laboratory for Coastal Research in Miami. The wide beach is composed of clean white sand, not powdery as on some Florida beaches, but still of fine quality. To walk south along the barrier strip that protects Nauset Marsh is to walk in a world stripped to its essential elements—sand, sea, and sky. "It really is a whole different world," says Sammartino. "I've never felt more free anywhere that I've been, and I grew up in the mountains of Colorado. It grabs ahold of your heartstrings."

South of Coast Guard Beach and Nauset Inlet runs a long barrier strip called Nauset Beach, the southern end of Cape Cod National Seashore. Unlike most of the park's beach, Nauset has an over-sand vehicle path open to use by locals, and it can get very busy in summer. Sammartino, who lives in the nearby town of Orleans, says, "On Fourth of July weekend you wouldn't find me out there for love nor money."

Numerous beach camps—one- or two-room buildings—dot Nauset. Built since the 1800s for fishing and recreation these "cultural treasures" as Sammartino calls them attest, like the dune shacks on the Cape's north end, to the interesting patchwork of ownership within park boundaries. The park bought some of the camps, while other owners worked out 25-year or lifelong leases. "A structure built before 1959 could opt out of this whole process and stay private in perpetuity," explains Sammartino. "Structures built after 1959 were considered speculative because there were rumblings about a park coming to town at that time."

Back on the carless stretch north of Coast Guard Beach, a highlights tour with Sammartino stops at Nauset Light Beach, where at low tide you can "get a sense for the impermanence of Cape Cod." With constant erosion, the original Three Sisters Lighthouses fell over the edge of the dune ridge; a second set was put out of commission in the 1920s when new technology—blinking patterns and colored

Waves wash the barnacled remains of an old dock at Herring Cove Beach, on the Cape's fist. A long stretch of beach to the north and south is popular with sunbathers and beachcombers.

Goslings huddle at the edge of Beech Forest Pond. Opposite, an elegant trio of pink lady's slippers blooms along the Beech Forest Trail. This native orchid is one of many wildflowers found at Cape Cod National Seashore.

TOURS WITH RANGERS

lights—made the group of three obsolete. Then in 1996 the single light was moved farther inland. Now, in a single snapshot of history, you can see the brick base of one of the Three Sisters, a post at the top of the bluff marking the spot where Nauset Light stood just nine years ago, and, back across the road, the lighthouse standing today, "hopefully safe for several more decades."

Sammartino outlines the Cape's glacial past and evanescent future in a simple way: "The Cape was formed by solid water, and it's going to be taken away by liquid water. And eventually there will be no more Cape Cod. There's a joke among locals: It doesn't matter where your house is. At some point you're bound to have waterfront property."

Continuing up along the Cape's forearm, the coastal bluff grows steeper and higher—up to 130 feet at the Highlands of North Truro. The Cape's first lighthouse was built here in 1797, commissioned by George Washington. High Head was the end of the Cape 6,000 years ago—the geologic "blink of an eye," according to Sammartino. The large dune area beyond—containing Provincetown and the entire curled fist of the Cape—accumulated in the last few thousand years by the longshore transport of oceanside sediments. "It's a very dramatic change when the upland suddenly drops off and you go down into this windblown dune environment," says Sammartino.

This is the area the Pilgrims saw when they first arrived in 1620. But they did not see what we see today, says Sammartino. "They were seeing beautiful forested areas. But they started cutting down those forests for shipbuilding and home-building and fires, and it turned out there was a very thin layer of topsoil. Underneath was just sand, and that sand started blowing." By the 1700s they had rules to keep people and livestock off the dunes, the remaining vegetation of which was keeping the sand from swallowing Provincetown. The Pilgrims came around and dropped anchor in Provincetown Harbor. They eventually ended up at Plymouth, though a few decided to return to Cape Cod and settled in current Eastham.

Most of the park lies on the ocean side of the Cape. The bay-side parts of Cape Cod National Seashore have a completely different character from the tumultuous drama of the ocean side. Even just beyond Provincetown, the salt marshes are places to find peace and quiet. A long breakwater or dike runs south from Provincetown and makes, says chief ranger Steve Prokop, a wonderful place to walk and get away from the bustle of town. There are wide views of bay, boats, and lighthouses. "You feel like you're at the end of the world."

Another bay-side place Prokop favors is Great Island, actually no longer an island but a peninsula connected to the Cape by a slender isthmus, known locally as a

On a foggy day the Cape Cod Light (or Highland Light) comes shining through. One of the brightest lights on the Atlantic Coast, its four-million-candle-power, double bull's-eye electric lamps are visible more than 20 miles out to sea on a clear day. In 1996 it was moved back from an eroding cliff.

tombolo. Prokop speaks fondly of the four-mile hike out to the tip of Great Island, and of using the outgoing tide to kayak to the island and then, when the tide turns, to get a free ride back a few hours later.

"Great Island was a major location for harvesting whales that were taken in Cape Cod Bay," says Prokop. Whale blubber was cooked on the island and rendered into oil. With the whale supply running low by the mid-19th century, the whaling industry began dying. "Now there's a big whaling industry for the tourist trade. Although you're more likely to see whales on an excursion, you don't have to take a boat out to see them. You might see a whale if you spend some time looking out over the horizon." Prokop has seen an occasional right whale, and more frequently humpback and pilot whales up at Race Point Beach, within a hundred yards of the shore. "The right whales will stay right on the surface. Their heads are huge, and they'll cruise along slowly."

Footprints in the sand carefully avoid vegetation in the parabolic dunes area on the Cape's wrist. Among the plants and animals finding footholds in this zone are the federally-listed threatened piping plover and the state-listed endangered oysterleaf.

Following pages: In the stillness at dawn, Ranger Tom Parsons paddles on the violet waters of Gull Pond near Wellfleet. One of more than 20 freshwater ponds in the seashore, this kettle pond was created by Ice Age glaciers; it is refreshed solely by precipitation.

Sandwiched between the bay and the ocean, Fort Hill overlooks the spectacular Nauset Marsh, where a trail leads into a birder's paradise. Prokop observes that from here one can almost tell the park boundary by the level of development right up to the edge. South and west of Fort Hill stand new homes; to the north and east spreads the salt marsh. "It's always a balancing act," he says. "Our number one mission is to protect the park's resources—natural, cultural, and historical."

For the time being development on the outer Cape is held in check by the park boundary. Wintertime also plays a hand in pruning back the population of this largely July-to-August seashore. The largest town on the Cape, Provincetown has a population of 35,000 in the summer, but it shrinks to about 3,500 in the winter. Likewise, the beach itself contracts seasonally on this mutable coastline. As Mark Adams explains, "The ocean does some amazing things in the winter. A lot of the beach sand gets mobilized off the shore, so the beaches get really carved out. In the summer the beach comes back." The winds and storms that scour the beaches can peel back layers of the Cape's past. "This spring we found a place where there were horse and cart-wheel tracks in the peat that was buried under the beach. It probably hadn't been exposed in fifty or a hundred years."

The find was made in Provincetown on the Cape's fist, an area created by shifting sands in the last 6,000 years. The whole north part of the Cape, as Jenna Sammartino points out, was formed by these same winds of change. She likes to stand, face to the wind, at the edge of this newly created piece of Cape Cod, where the Highlands plummet to the Cape's thin wrist. To windward the vastness of the Atlantic spreads limitless and compelling.

"You get the feeling you're standing on the edge of the continent," she says. "Thoreau chose to finish his book on Cape Cod with the simple sentence that a man may stand there and put all America behind him. It's so true—you're standing on the edge. When I do my programs on the beach I generally start by asking people why they come to the beach, and I love all the varied answers that I get. Kids want to build sand castles, teenagers want to surf, the adults are just trying to get some peace and quiet. It doesn't really matter what your reason is; the point is that for some reason the seashore, the sea's edge, holds an intrinsic value for all of us."

Seashores

"Many people refer to OLYMPIC NATIONAL PARK as three parks in one," says ranger Mike Guerling. "It has a coastal area, mountains, and a temperate rain forest ecosystem." Encompassing much of Washington's Olympic Peninsula, this spectacularly diverse park has a rugged Pacific shore, a temperate rain forest, and a mountain system that itself includes subalpine forest, alpine meadows, and snow-capped peaks. Each ecosystem supports a healthy population of wildlife: Sea otters swim off the coast; salmon spawn in the clear mountain streams; deer graze in the alpine meadows.

After 17 years, Guerling has scouted out several places in Olympic that he considers special. Along the coast, he likes Shi Shi Beach in the northwest corner of the park, just south of the Makah Indian Reservation. It's not one of the easiest places to get to, but once there you have a three-mile deserted beach haunted by driftwood, coastal fog, brown bears, and seastacks. "At very low tide you can walk into the caves and arches at Point of Arches," says Guerling. "Because the exposure is so great you can see intertidal plants and animals you can't see anywhere else along the coast."

OLYMPIC NATIONAL PARK

Another great stretch of unpopulated coast lies to the south at Toleak, below the Quileute Reservation. "To me it's like a sacred place," says Guerling. "For a thousand years or more, the Quileute Indians used it as a summer encampment site, and along the banks you find middens with whalebones and clamshells."

In the rain forest zone, Guerling likes to get away to a wilderness trail south of the main Hoh Valley. It follows the South Fork of the Hoh River up into the park. The moss and ancient trees dampen almost all sound. "It's very quiet unless you're there during a rainstorm or if the wind's blowing. Sometimes the wind is almost like a train, a deafening whoosh in the tops of the trees." Even on still days he has heard giants crashing to the ground. "It's a pretty amazing thing to hear—we're talking about trees that are 250 to 300 feet high."

In the mountainous area, Guerling is partial to a 44-mile trail from Whisky Bend to the North Fork of the Quinault River via the Elwha Valley. "You're right in the center of the park, in the center of the peninsula. Of the three to four million people who visit the park every year, very few people take that trail." Guerling and his wife hiked the entire trail a few years ago, and during the six-day trek they encountered only two other people. "It's such an isolated wilderness area. You're seeing what it has looked like since the Ice Age 10,000 years ago, with the exception of a few bridges and the trail."

Just north of San Francisco, POINT REYES NATIONAL SEASHORE also boasts a great diversity of landscapes and flora and fauna. Different layers of soil, created by plate tectonics, combine with the area's temperate climate to support a rich variety of plant communities found in few other regions of the continent.

Ranger John Dell'Osso, a 21-year park veteran who grew up in the Bay area, finds that diversity

POINT REYES NATIONAL SEASHORE

particularly striking along Limantour Beach at the south end of the peninsula. "It's a popular beach, but the surrounding area includes both fresh- and saltwater marshes," says Dell'Osso. "It descends down a fir-lined ridge and comes through coastal scrub and finally into the grasslands and marshlands. So there's a real diversity of habitat out that way." He explains that Limantour is also part of an area that was being parceled off and sold in the 1950s, giving the Sierra Club and local politicians impetus to push the National Park Service to purchase the land.

Up at the north end of the park lies Tomales Point, an area that Dell'Osso calls "spectacular." A trail up a high windswept promontory yields views of the Pacific Ocean on one side and Tomales Bay on the other. Wildflowers grow rampant in spring and summer, and tule elk graze there year-round. "The tule elk were native to the area, but probably extinct locally for over a hundred years," says Dell'Osso. Reintroduced in 1978, the small elk have grown from a herd of 10 to 450; to slow the population growth, some elk have been moved to the wilderness at Limantour.

Dell'Osso likes to point out that in addition to its obvious natural beauty, Point Reyes has had a steady stream of human history for more than 5,000 years, starting with the Coast Miwok Indians, continuing with the wave of European explorers, and culminating with ranchers who started here in the 1850s. The cattle ranches, leased back from the government, still quilt the park landscape. And the Miwok history "is still very much alive today with the local tribe that we work closely with," says Dell'Osso.

Saw palmettos catch the westering sun amid saw grass and pine trees on the east side of Everglades National Park. The park's great abundance and diversity of habitat and wildlife all depend on reliable flows of fresh water.

CHAPTER 6

A Vanishing Paradise

The Everglades spread across the tip of the Florida peninsula in waves of green and gold—vast plains of saw grass dotted with islands like ships in a verdant sea. On and on the Everglades run, down to the spindly mangroves that gird the broken coastline. An immense sky overarches the entire scene, an azure canvas for billowing clouds that can stack up like alpine ranges in the summertime. Especially lovely in the soft, bent light of dawn and dusk, the estuaries and saw-grass plains have a simple, primal quality.

The mind grasps for metaphors of sea and mountains because this is an area like no other in the United States. Encompassing 1.5 million acres, Everglades National Park—itself less than half the entire Everglades ecosystem—contains the largest expanse of unsullied landscape in the Southeast. More than 85 percent of its acreage is designated as wilderness. An ark of rare birds, reptiles, and mammals, the park stretches more than 60 miles north to south, 40 east to west. Among the endangered species finding a foothold here are Florida panthers, manatees, wood storks, Cape Sable seaside sparrows, and American crocodiles. With the largest continuous stand of saw-grass prairie in the continent, the park is recognized as a World Heritage Site, an International Biosphere Reserve, and a Wetland of International Importance. Fast growing populations in Miami and Naples have put the Everglades and its wildlife in serious jeopardy in recent decades. Some rangers tend to dwell on the problems, others on the beauty remaining.

Except for a two-year hiatus, ranger Maureen McGee-Ballinger has been with Everglades National Park since 1992. She knows its varying climates, seasons, environments; she has seen its many moods. Yet she would be the first to admit that she has not seen it all, that the Everglades can deliver a nearly inexhaustible number of sights and experiences. She has never, for instance, seen a panther—probably the rarest mammal in the country. But she has witnessed an enviable list of wonders, great and small. And she has an eye for details that might escape the notice of the casual visitor.

Fragrant water lilies bloom along the park's canoe trails. Some 700 plant species live in the Everglades, as well as 300 bird species, the endangered manatee, crocodile, and Florida panther.

McGee-Ballinger will not readily admit to favorite places, claiming that each place is special for different reasons. Instead, she likes to talk of her favorite season—winter, or, in Everglades-speak, the dry season. "That's when you see the most wildlife," she says, "because you have a dry-down. The animals that have been spread out over the Glades follow the water. That's where the food is, the shelter. That's the comfort zone for a lot of the creatures here. They concentrate at the water holes. That's part of what makes the Everglades so amazing."

What would she do with an entire free day to spend in the Everglades? "If I was coming in at daybreak in the winter, I'd start with a slow trek between the entrance station and Royal Palm, because there's often beautiful mist or dew on the spiderwebs, and they cover everything in the saw grass. It's like acres of jewels. Then I'd go out on the Anhinga Trail, because if it was cool overnight alligators and turtles would be coming out of the water to warm up in the morning sun.

Its darting beak ready for duty, a great blue heron stalks through Shark Valley in search of small fish, amphibians, and even baby alligators. Great white herons sometimes breed with great blues, and are thus members of the same species. Herons fold their necks into an "S" shape when in flight.

Following pages: Red mangroves growing near Flamingo, in the southern part of the park, appear to walk on their multiple roots. The hearty salt-extruding mangrove is vital to the health of the south Florida coast: It acts as a coastal buffer, shelters and feeds shrimp and other aquatic life, and helps stabilize coastal land.

The turtles might munch on the water lilies. And if the willows are blooming, birds like the purple gallinule might be feeding on those flowers." As McGee-Ballinger points out, there is an endless number of discoveries to be made here. "It's only a half-mile trail, but I can easily spend an hour to two hours there, no problem. It's one of those trails, when you walk around your half-mile, you look up, then you can walk it again and see different things. It's constantly changing."

The Gumbo-Limbo is more off the beaten track than the Anhinga. The trail penetrates a lush subtropical garden of ferns, wild coffee, and air orchids, rank jungly odors blending with luxuriant perfumes. Temperate climate hardwoods like live oak and sumac mix with tropicals such as the gumbo-limbo, with its trademark "sunburned" red skin. The birds are always active, particularly around the edges of the Gumbo-Limbo Trail, which is the edge of a hammock.

The next place she would stop is the pinelands, an entirely different habitat. "It's a fire-dependent environment," McGee-Ballinger observes. "In the summer we don't just get rain, we get thunderstorms. They set off fires, the fires burn out the competition, and the pine trees thrive. In places where they don't burn, the scrub grows up, and it'll become a hammock. I like to get into the pinelands in the wintertime because that's when you're more likely to spot tree snails. You have to look very carefully. They can be very tiny, or they can be a couple of inches long. In the winter, because it's the dry season and a snail needs moisture, they seal themselves to the trees to conserve their moisture. They're not moving around very much and you're more likely to spot one. They're very colorful—they can be white or yellow; I have seen browns, greens. Some have pink tips on the ends of the spiral, some have brown-and-yellow bands. And with all that color, it's still a challenge to find them. The colors help them blend in, particularly in a place like the pinelands where you've got sun filtering through vegetation. The light is very dappled."

When asked about the snail kite—a rare Everglades bird—McGee-Ballinger makes a distinction, and at the same time an offhand reference to amazing things she has observed. "The kites don't go for the tree snails. They go for apple snails. You tend to see more snail kites up around Shark Valley where you have the larger flow of the Shark River Slough. I've seen them grab an apple snail. It's not an easy thing because the snail stays underwater most of the time—the birds have to glide

Sunrise encrimsons the pinelands in the eastern Everglades (above), giving it the look of an African savanna. The shell of a freshwater apple snail (below) lies on the floor of the pinelands. The rare hawk-like snail kite feeds almost exclusively on these snails.

over and watch carefully to find a snail near the surface and grab it. Tree snails don't interest them. Sometimes in the winter if a crow spots a tree snail, and it's sitting on the tree for a few months at a time, then the crow will try to peck through the shell. But generally it's not worth their effort."

By midday of her busman's holiday, McGee-Ballinger would be getting into the dwarf cypress forest. "They're deciduous conifers," she explains, "so it's pretty cool, because in winter they've dropped all their needles, yet you see cones on them. A lot of times people will go through there and it looks confusing—*Did the whole forest die? Is there a problem with the area?* So it creates a kind of silvery forest."

Within this area stands one of her favorite overlooks, a quintessential, horizon-to-horizon Everglades viewpoint called Pay-hay-okee, a Seminole word for "grassy waters." "It's a tremendous view. You can see the dwarf cypress trees, and the saw-grass prairie, and you can even get a feel for how the Taylor Slough starts to curve out toward the Gulf of Mexico."

With enthusiasm radiating from everything McGee-Ballinger says, one would think she had her eyes on a ranger job long ago. In fact, after earning an under-graduate degree at Southern Illinois University, she was headed for a career in law. The turning point came during a summer stint at Yellowstone. "I got hooked," she says. "I looked around and discovered that I could work in places like that. So I dropped the law career and did my best to get myself in the park service." Her first paid position was at the Jefferson National Expansion Memorial in St. Louis; she later worked at Independence National Historical Park in Philadelphia. A back-ground in history helped in those parks. "But when I switched to a more natural setting," she explains, "there was more on-the-ground learning."

After several years in the Everglades, she missed mountains and snow enough to move to the opposite corner of the country—Mount Rainier National Park. "Then I missed the alligators and the crocodiles, so I came back to the Everglades. What really drew me back here was the subtropical environment. This is the only place in the United States where you can see native crocodiles. You have alligators, snakes, turtles, a myriad of fish, both freshwater and saltwater, and the different habitats. This is not like the Grand Canyon or Half Dome—this is a place where you have to walk a little slower, look a little closer. It's a place of subtleties."

After Pay-hay-okee, McGee-Ballinger would take time out to explore Mahogany Hammock. In this humid jungle, the nation's largest mahogany trees grow, filtering meager shards of sunlight. Zebra but-terflies flit by rare orchids—prized by collectors and poachers—and strangler figs wrap around host trees in a slow but deadly embrace. "It's darker and damper in the hammock, and a little cooler," says McGee-Ballinger. "The ferns thrive.

An anhinga poses, appropriately, along the Anhinga Trail. The bird uses its dagger beak to spear fish under water, then deftly tosses the prey into its mouth; it later finds a dry perch to dry its wings in the sun. The anhinga is nicknamed "snakebird" for its habit of swimming with only its head and neck showing.

And there is a huge beautiful mahogany tree right next to the trail, and wonderful palms, oaks, and air plants. There's a ball moss which looks like somebody took some Spanish moss, rolled it up into a ball, and stuck it into a tree. The trail has some elevation, so you can get a feel for what it's like to be halfway up into the canopy."

She might stop next at Paurotis Pond, a favorite nesting place for wood storks and roseate spoonbills. Or just south at Nine Mile Pond, a great loop canoe trail. By the end of the dry season parts of the trail are simply too dry to paddle, but it's a good way to see both saw grass and mangrove: "It's a transition zone between

TOURS WITH RANGERS

A salt-marsh pink (opposite) blooms in the pinelands area, while small mangroves (above)
form a sunset tableau near Paurotis Pond. Few plants other than the
mangrove can survive in salty brackish water.

Flared trunks of bald cypress make reflective patterns in Big Cypress Swamp, bordering the north side of the park. The deciduous conifers, relatives of the sequoia and redwood, shed their needles in winter. Logged extensively for their rot-resistant wood, bald cypresses now live primarily in southeastern preserves.

TOURS WITH RANGERS

the fresh and salt areas." Or nearby West Lake, with mangroves "all the way around the trail, so you're going through a tunnel of mangrove."

On the other hand, she might just hurry on down to Flamingo, where she is currently stationed. "I've been out in Whitewater Bay and Coot Bay and had dolphins jumping right next to my boat. I've stood in front of Flamingo Visitor Center looking out into the bay and seen dolphins feeding right out there. The waterways here are fantastic, and if you get into a canoe or kayak you can be out for three or four hours and have a very solitary, beautiful experience. The vast majority of this park is underwater a good part of the year, so a canoe or kayak or boat is the only way to get out there. On an overnight trip you can get deep into the backcountry." McGee-Ballinger also likes the Snake Bight Trail from Flamingo, because it's one of the very few long-distance walking trails in the park. "It can be mosquitoey through the mangrove, but after two and a half miles you get down to the Florida Bay edge and you might see flamingos."

Given another day, McGee-Ballinger would focus on the northern parts of the park. A convoluted maze of emerald mangrove islets, the Ten Thousand Islands area forms an ideal haven for manatees, dolphins, ospreys, terns, cormorants, herons, and roseate spoonbills. "And I've seen magnificent frigate birds up there—huge gorgeous black birds. And there's a neat canoeing trail which crosses between Everglades and Big Cypress. And I would definitely head over to Shark Valley—the wildlife there is tremendous." The Shark River Slough there winds around mangroves and slowly flows from central Florida through the Everglades. Views are sometimes limited by profligate saw grass, which can grow up to 12 feet tall. But a viewing tower stands as a reward at the far end of a 15-mile loop road. "I've been out there in the summer and seen amazing thunderstorms in the distance. Sometimes not in the distance."

Another angle on Everglades National Park comes at nighttime. "On the Anhinga Trail, if it's a cool evening, reptiles love to come out on the paved part because it acts like a big hot rock. You often hear the frogs singing at night. The eyes of animals cast different reflective lights at night—greens and reds. Owls will come out. They're silent—you don't hear them flying, but sometimes they'll swoop right past you and grab something. I also like to go to the end of the trail and watch the stars reflected in the water. If it's a calm night it's hard to tell where the sky ends and the water begins."

When told how wonderful it is to see the park through her eyes, McGee-Ballinger responds that the best part of her job is seeing the park through people who have never been there before. "Everything is new," she says. "Everything's an adventure. And children

A canoeist (opposite) prepares to head out on a trail on Nine Mile Pond, in the south part of the park.
Above, ranger Adam Friedrich pulls canoes through shallow areas of a mangrove swamp in April, before
the wet season has returned. Head nets provide mosquito protection.

An alligator bellows a territorial warning along a trail in Shark Valley. Alligators often take to the sun to warm their bodies. A descendant of dinosaurs, the American alligator feeds but once or twice a week. Once hunted relentlessly for their hides, they have made a comeback under federal and state protection.

are terrific because nothing stops them, nothing slows them down." Clearly, the park experience for McGee-Ballinger is about people encountering the beauty of the natural world.

Park ranger Stephen Robinson has a somewhat different outlook. He has worked at Everglades every winter season for the past 26 years. A fourth-generation Floridian, he grew up in central Florida. His fondest memories are of exploring the wetlands in his grandfather's hand-hewn wooden boats using cypress poles. He describes his grandfather as an optimist. "But he stood there one day and said, 'This is not the same scene I saw when I was your age. There was no development, no drainage.'"

Those words haunted Robinson when he grew older. "So I came to the Everglades with the concept that I want to see what my granddad saw. I want to see those original things. I'm going to go down where it's protected forever." Yet down in presumably the last vestige of true Florida wilderness, he encountered a similarly vanishing paradise. Boat captains and others who had been there for 20 years said it was not the same place they had known. One was so disheartened he had stopped taking private tours. "What was missing overwhelmed what was left," Robinson explains.

Ask Robinson what his favorite places are in the Everglades and he cannot refrain from passionately detailing how the Everglades works and does not work. Indeed, the complex web of environmental and political issues surrounding the region—the subject of numerous books—is probably more at the forefront of this national park than any other. To study the issues, Everglades has the largest science staff of any national park—80 to 90 people.

In short, the problem is water. The Everglades' wonderful variety of plant and animal life depends upon a wide, shallow current, which until the 1920s flowed unrestricted from Lake Okeechobee to Florida Bay. To service a booming South Florida population, the U.S. Army Corps of Engineers built some 1,400 miles of canals in the mid-1900s. But birds and other animals began disappearing in masses. The billions of gallons siphoned off the Everglades annually has reduced the original ecosystem by half. Where a million alligators once thrived, there are now a few thousand; a quarter million wading birds have declined to less than 20,000. The Corps has embarked on an ambitious, and costly, restoration plan to replumb the entire system using underground reservoirs that periodically release water and thus imitate the natural wet and dry cycles of the Glades. Whether this 30-year project will work on such a large scale is the subject of much debate.

Robinson is one of many who have their doubts that big machines can imitate natural systems. Yet he continues to return to the Everglades for "the same reason people hung in there at the Alamo. You try not to give up. I really believe we could trade off the sugarcane farming for a healthy ecosystem in South Florida and the protection of the people that live there and the fisheries. The survival of the people and the Everglades are one and the same. It's just a matter of when political wisdom catches up with natural history and science."

When pressed on his favorite things to do in the park, he admits to canoe-sailing and paddling, but with caveats. First of all, the main waterways are exempt from the wilderness restrictions, so powerboats are allowed in. Finding serenity is getting harder and harder. "I use incoming tides in Florida Bay and two inches of water," he says. "That keeps the powerboats away. Then I can get out there with the wading birds and the little baby sharks swimming across the flats. But it's hard to schedule that—it takes local knowledge of the shifting tides and the wind, as well as luck, to get all the conditions right. Wetlands are inconvenient, especially for people with a limited amount of time."

He also likes wading through the marshy areas. "When the Everglades is flowing, it's almost crystal clear, and wading through it you come out with your shoes cleaner than when you went in. That's kind of a hoot. But for most of the season that's not the case—there's not a healthy flow. You're just walking through mud."

Another of his favorite activities is likewise tinged with sadness. Sailing into Florida Bay at sunset and watching the evening migration of ibis and egrets and other birds from the mainland to the islands is a shadow of its former glory. There were once flights of thousands of birds, and in Robinson's early years in the park he saw flights of 500; now there are groups of 20 to 50. "It still happens," he says. "The remaining super-birds that are able to fly farther and work harder and try new creative things—they still try to keep the basic pattern of roosting at night, getting away from bobcats and possums. It goes on, but it's hardly as awe-inspiring as it was in the '80s."

Yet Robinson, who spends his summers as a ranger at Crater Lake National Park, refuses to give up on the Everglades. "It's definitely a place every nature lover should experience," he insists. "You should not get so upset you never have fun. But it's not Disney World. More and more college kids go there on spring break—they're trying to learn and not just get drunk." He compares visiting the Everglades with visiting somebody in the hospital: "You're not a surgeon, you can't fix them, but you love them and you go there and try to give them support, try to find out what the situation is. People want to show love to the Everglades and they want to get love back. That's possible, but not without understanding it. A lot is required of the visitor."

Avid birders from British Columbia (above) scan for interesting sightings at Eco Pond, including laughing gulls (below), which live primarily along the southeast coast. The tremendous variety of birdlife in the Everglades has long attracted visitors—a century ago they came to hunt plumes, now they come to watch.

Another seasonal ranger, Adam Friedrich grew up backpacking in the Sierra Nevada. He has spent only one season at the Everglades, hence he brings a fresh perspective. While working on a degree in natural resource interpretation at Humboldt State University in northern California, he took up surfing and kayaking. Those skills looked good on his resume when he applied for a job in the Everglades. But he was in for a surprise upon arrival.

"My first reaction when I got to the Everglades was, *What did I get myself into?* You drive across the park and you see absolutely nothing. It looks very monotonous; you expect to see giraffes and zebras running around in that topography. Then I started to see what the park had to offer. If you slow down you start to notice things. The wildlife diversity is just amazing. I had never seen an alligator in my life. And here there were crocodiles out my back door." Small things, too, called out for attention. "A little spider caught my eye on the bird walk at Eco Pond one day. It was the strangest looking spider I'd ever seen in my life. I looked it up—it was called a crab-legged spiny orb weaver. You just stumble on things like that here."

Even in a six-month stint he beheld some spectacular things. "I used to like going down to Snake Bight. One day I happened to see something pink in the mangroves way off. I got closer and closer and it turned out it was about 20 roseate spoonbills. Then I got a little too close and spooked them, and there were actually more like a hundred." Adam also is fond of the morning canoe trips he guided out on Nine Mile Pond. "We'd be out three to four hours with about six boats. We'd go through the mangrove tunnels and see a lot of alligators and the same crocodile every time." He mentions that the Nine Mile canoe trail is basically "a series of holes in the ground that they dynamited to get the limestone out so they could build up the road."

That inevitably leads to a discussion of area road building and its effect on the park. Along with drainage to urban areas, major east-west highways act like tourniquets, choking off the water into the park. "What we get now is about a third of the historic waterflow. Those highways are just big dams." Friedrich compares the Everglades to Yellowstone, where he has worked the past four summers. "Yellowstone was set aside so long ago there weren't any resource issues. They've pretty well restored the ecosystem there. But the Everglades wasn't set aside until the late '40s, and everything was already developing. Now, by the end of the winter with the water running low, the alligators start running out of food and they begin

A boat wake ripples the water in the Ten Thousand Islands off Chokoloskee Bay. The number of islands, though far less than 10,000, continues to change as mangroves build up into landmasses that then, with storms and tides, break apart. Islands range in size from a few trees to several hundred acres.

looking at each other. They'll cannibalize one another if it gets bad enough."

The rangers of Everglades will agree that it is a park in peril. They would also agree that there is still a glimmer of hope for restoring it to at least a vestige of its early 20th-century appearance. In the meantime, they'll tell you, there are still wonders to behold throughout the park, wonders that reveal themselves slowly. Such wonders make their own case for saving the park.

Swamps

Preserving the largest intact expanse of old-growth floodplain forest in the country, CONGAREE NATIONAL PARK in South Carolina has been designated an International Biosphere Reserve. In this waterlogged woodland, giant loblolly pines and hardwoods rise to a canopy higher than in the Amazon rain forest. Loblolly pines thrust up 150 to 170 feet to reach the sunlight, and some majestic old bald cypresses measure more than 25 feet in circumference, their leafy crown shuttering the world below into a landscape of liquid shades of brown and green. Swagged by Spanish moss and surrounded by a company of knobby knees, the bald cypress rises from dark water to a tapered waist, a twisted trunk, and a sky full of branches with feathery leaves. This deciduous conifer is a symbol of the vanishing southeastern wetlands.

Park naturalist Fran Remetta has been with Congaree since 1980, and still one of his favorite places is the Low Boardwalk Trail, which loops 2.5 miles through a grove of old-growth tupelo and bald cypress trees. He particularly admires the overlook of Weston Lake, where fanlike dwarf palmettos just off the walk lend a tropical accent to the surroundings. River otters frolic in the oxbow lake, and red-bellied turtles line up on floating logs. Some innocuous-looking floating sticks turn out to be gar, fish with razor-sharp teeth. The occasional great blue heron flaps by, and belted kingfishers rocket past. In summer a resident alligator sometimes shows itself, but not even Remetta knows where it goes in winter.

Remetta says that the forest used to flood about ten times a year, but a recent five-year drought has made the flooding unpredictable. When heavy rains do fall, the low boardwalk lies underwater. "But on the elevated boardwalk you can still walk over the floodwaters. You get the feeling of being on an island, because it's surrounded by water."

"My favorite time of day," says Remetta, "is just before dusk. The rays of the sun highlight the tall trees, and there's a distinctive line that separates the glowing golden crowns of the trees and the dark bases beneath." He also likes nighttime, especially when he's leading an "owl prowl." The eerie hoots of barred owls and the glowing of fungi on the cypresses deepen the mystery of an already primitive landscape.

Down in Florida's BIG CYPRESS NATIONAL PRESERVE, sweeping vistas of wet prairies extend to far horizons punctuated with hardwood hammocks; panthers prowl in soggy forests under broad-skirted cypresses that stood before Christopher

Columbus was born; mangrove thickets shelter fish near the broken islands of the Everglades. The 729,000-acre preserve protects nearly half of the remaining Big Cypress ecosystem, buffering the Everglades on the north.

Ranger Bob DeGrosse likes walking along the 37 miles of the Florida National Scenic Trail that lie within the preserve. "The southernmost section of the preserve is a very interesting place to walk in the dry season," he says. "It goes through everything from open prairies to cypress and pine forests. And around March and April it's a good place to see flowering plants, including terrestrial orchids and bromeliads."

BIG CYPRESS NATIONAL PRESERVE

Even just going a short distance in lets you experience the beauty and solitude of the preserve, maintains DeGrosse. "Because it's a swamp habitat a lot of people are reticent to get off the road, but when you do you really only have to get off a couple of hundred yards and you feel as if you're in a remote wild area." Among the wildlife you sometimes see are white-tailed deer and black bear. "You might see signs of a panther," says DeGrosse of the elusive and rare creatures who have made a last stand in these parts. DeGrosse has been lucky enough to see them, usually around dawn.

A simple way to get a taste for the area, says DeGrosse, is to stop at some of the new boardwalks and wildlife viewing platforms at and near the visitor center on the Tamiami Trail, the highway from Naples to Miami. The boardwalk west of the visitor center, he says, is a particularly good place to get into the heart of a cypress stand. And migrating songbirds are easily visible here in spring and fall.

DeGrosse also points to the Loop Road, a 27-mile gravel drive, as a good place to see a variety of wildlife. And he's fond of bicycling in the Bear Island area in the northwest corner of the preserve, and canoeing on the Turner River near where it slides into Everglades National Park.

When asked about orchid thieves in Big Cypress, DeGrosse admits that, alas, poachers continue to prey on everything from orchids and saw palmettos to tree snails, alligators, and snakes. "South Florida has a lot of flora and fauna not found anywhere else in the continental United States. So a lot of collectors come down here."

MORE PARKS OF INTEREST

This list includes some of the more than 300 properties managed by the National Park Service. For a more complete listing and further information, visit www.nps.gov.

ACADIA NATIONAL PARK: BAR HARBOR, ME
Points of interest: Endangered Species · Mountains · Wildflowers · Wildlife Viewing · Biking · Boating · Camping · Climbing · Fishing · Hiking · Horseback Riding · Swimming · Snow Skiing

ADAMS NATIONAL HISTORICAL PARK: QUINCY, MA
Points of interest: American Presidents · Civil War · Revolutionary War · Westward Expansion

AGATE FOSSIL BEDS NATIONAL MONUMENT: HARRISON, NE
Points of interest: Fossils/Dinosaurs · Wildflowers · Wildlife Viewing · Fishing · Hiking

APPALACHIAN NATIONAL SCENIC TRAIL: MAINE TO GEORGIA
Points of interest: Wildlife Viewing · Camping · Fishing · Hiking · Wilderness Area

ARCHES NATIONAL PARK: MOAB, UT
Points of interest: Wildflowers · Biking · Camping · Climbing · Hiking

BADLANDS NATIONAL PARK: SOUTHWESTERN SD
Points of interest: Fossils/Dinosaurs · Wildflowers · Wildlife Viewing · Biking · Camping · Hiking · Horseback Riding · Wilderness Area

BERING LAND BRIDGE NATIONAL PRESERVE: NOME, AK
Points of interest: Wildlife Viewing · Fossils/Dinosaurs · Geysers/Hot Springs · Volcanoes · Wildflowers · Westward Expansion · Boating · Camping · Fishing · Hiking · Hunting · Snow Skiing

BIG BEND NATIONAL PARK: BIG BEND NATIONAL PARK, TX
Points of interest: Endangered Species · Wildlife Viewing · Fossils/Dinosaurs · Mountains · Volcanoes · Wildflowers · Boating · Fishing

BISCAYNE NATIONAL PARK: HOMESTEAD, FL
Points of interest: Coral Reefs · Endangered Species · Wildlife Viewing · Maritime History · Boating · Camping · Fishing · Hiking · Swimming

CANYONLANDS NATIONAL PARK: MOAB, UT
Points of interest: Wildlife Viewing · Hiking · Camping

CARLSBAD CAVERNS NATIONAL PARK: CARLSBAD, NM
Points of interest: Wildlife Viewing · Caves · Fossils/ Dinosaurs · Hiking

CRATER LAKE NATIONAL PARK: CRATER LAKE, OR
Points of interest: Wildlife Viewing · Geysers/Hot Springs · Volcanoes · Biking · Camping · Fishing · Hiking · Wilderness Area

DEATH VALLEY NATIONAL PARK: DEATH VALLEY, CA, NV
Points of interest: Early Explorers · Endangered Species · Wildlife Viewing · Fossils/Dinosaurs · Geysers/Hot Springs · Mountains · Volcanoes · Wildflowers · Westward Expansion · Biking · Camping · Hiking · Horseback Riding · Swimming

DENALI NATIONAL PARK & PRESERVE: DENALI PARK, AK
Points of interest: Glaciers · Mountains · Wildlife Viewing · Biking · Camping · Climbing · Fishing · Hiking · Snow Skiing

DRY TORTUGAS NATIONAL PARK: KEY WEST, FL
Points of interest: Coral Reefs · Boating · Camping · Fishing · Swimming

GATES OF THE ARCTIC NATIONAL PARK & PRESERVE: BETTLES, AK
Points of interest: Wildlife Viewing · Boating · Camping · Climbing · Fishing · Hiking · Hunting · Snow Skiing

GLACIER BAY NATIONAL PARK & PRESERVE: GUSTAVUS, AK
Points of interest: Wildlife Viewing · Boating · Camping · Fishing · Hiking · Hunting

GLACIER NATIONAL PARK: NORTHWESTERN MONTANA, MT
Points of interest: Biking · Boating · Camping · Fishing · Hiking · Horseback Riding

GRAND CANYON NATIONAL PARK: GRAND CANYON, AZ
Points of interest: Wildlife Viewing · Biking · Boating · Camping · Fishing · Hiking · Horseback Riding

GRAND TETON NATIONAL PARK: MOOSE, WY
Points of interest: Wildlife Viewing · Biking · Boating · Camping · Climbing · Fishing · Hiking · Horseback Riding

GREAT BASIN NATIONAL PARK: BAKER, NV
Points of interest: Wildlife Viewing · Biking · Camping · Fishing · Hiking · Horseback Riding · Wilderness Area

GREAT SAND DUNES NATIONAL PARK & PRESERVE: MOSCA, CO
Points of interest: Wildlife Viewing · Camping · Climbing · Fishing · Hiking · Horseback Riding

GREAT SMOKY MOUNTAINS NATIONAL PARK: NC, TN
Points of interest: Wildlife Viewing · Biking · Camping · Fishing · Hiking · Horseback Riding

GUADALUPE MOUNTAINS NATIONAL PARK: SALT FLAT, TX
Points of interest: Wildlife Viewing · Camping · Hiking · Horseback Riding · Wilderness Area

HALEAKALA NATIONAL PARK: KULA, MAUI, HI
Points of interest: Wildlife Viewing · Camping · Hiking ·
Horseback Riding · Swimming · Wilderness Area

HAWAII VOLCANOES NATIONAL PARK: HILO, HAWAII, HI
Points of interest: Wildlife Viewing · Camping · Hiking ·
Hunting · Wilderness Area

HOT SPRINGS NATIONAL PARK: HOT SPRINGS, AR
Points of interest: Camping · Hiking · Horseback Riding

KATMAI NATIONAL PARK & PRESERVE: KING SALMON, AK
Points of interest: Wildlife Viewing · Glaciers · Volcanoes ·
Boating · Camping · Climbing · Fishing · Hiking · Hunting ·
Wilderness Area · Snow Skiing

KENAI FJORDS NATIONAL PARK: SEWARD, AK
Points of interest: Wildlife Viewing · Glaciers · Mountains ·
Wildflowers · Boating · Camping · Fishing · Hiking

MAMMOTH CAVE NATIONAL PARK: MAMMOTH CAVE, KY
Points of interest: Caves · Endangered Species · Wildflowers ·
Boating · Camping · Fishing · Hiking · Horseback Riding

MESA VERDE NATIONAL PARK: CORTEZ AND MANCOS, CO
Points of interest: Camping · Hiking · Wildlife Viewing

MOUNT RAINIER NATIONAL PARK:
ASHFORD, ENUMCLAW, PACKWOOD, WILKESON, WA
Points of interest: Wildlife Viewing · Geysers/Hot Springs ·
Glaciers · Volcanoes · Wildflowers · Biking · Camping ·
Climbing · Fishing · Hiking · Horseback Riding · Snow Skiing

NORTH CASCADES NATIONAL PARK: MARBLEMOUNT, WA
Points of interest: Endangered Species · Wildlife Viewing ·
Glaciers · Mountains · Biking · Boating · Camping · Climbing
· Fishing · Hiking · Horseback Riding · Wilderness Area

REDWOOD NATIONAL AND STATE PARKS:
DEL NORTE & HUMBOLDT COUNTIES, CA
Points of interest: Mountains · Wildlife Viewing ·
Biking · Boating · Camping · Fishing · Hiking · Horseback
Riding · Swimming · Wilderness Area

ROCKY MOUNTAIN NATIONAL PARK:
ESTES PARK AND GRAND LAKE, CO
Points of interest: Mountains · Wildlife Viewing ·
Biking · Camping · Climbing · Fishing · Hiking · Horseback
Riding · Wilderness Area · Snow Skiing

SHENANDOAH NATIONAL PARK:
BLUE RIDGE MOUNTAINS NEAR LURAY, VA
Points of interest: Mountains · Wildflowers · Wildlife Viewing ·Biking · Camping · Climbing · Fishing · Hiking · Horseback Riding · Wilderness Area

TALLGRASS PRAIRIE NATIONAL PRESERVE: STRONG CITY, KS
Points of interest: Early Explorers · Endangered Species · Wildflowers · Wildlife Viewing · Westward Expansion · Hiking

VIRGIN ISLANDS NATIONAL PARK: ST.JOHN, VI
Points of interest: Coral Reefs · Endangered Species ·
Boating · Camping · Fishing · Hiking · Swimming

VOYAGEURS NATIONAL PARK:
INTERNATIONAL FALLS, KABETOGAMA,
ASH RIVER, AND CRANE LAKE, MN
Points of interest: Wildlife Viewing · Glaciers · Westward
Expansion · Boating · Camping · Fishing · Hiking ·
Swimming · Wildlife Viewing · Snow Skiing

WRANGELL - ST ELIAS NATIONAL PARK & PRESERVE:
COPPER CENTER, AK
Points of interest: Wildlife Viewing · Glaciers · Mountains ·
Volcanoes · Wildflowers · Westward Expansion · Biking ·
Boating · Camping · Climbing · Fishing · Hiking · Horseback
Riding · Hunting · Snow Skiing

YELLOWSTONE NATIONAL PARK: ID, MT, WY
Points of interest: Endangered Species · Wildlife Viewing ·
Geysers/Hot Springs · Volcanoes · Westward Expansion ·
Biking · Boating · Camping · Climbing · Fishing · Hiking ·
Horseback Riding · Swimming · Wilderness Area · Snow Skiing

YUKON - CHARLEY RIVERS NATIONAL PRESERVE: EAGLE, AK
Points of interest: Wildlife Viewing · Fossils/Dinosaurs ·
Westward Expansion · Boating · Camping · Fishing · Hiking ·
Hunting · Snow Skiing

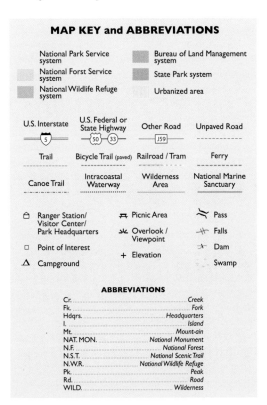

MAP KEY and ABBREVIATIONS

National Park Service system
Bureau of Land Management system
National Forst Service system
State Park system
National Wildlife Refuge system
Urbanized area

U.S. Interstate — 5 —
U.S. Federal or State Highway — 50 — 33 —
Other Road — J59 —
Unpaved Road - - - - - -

Trail
Bicycle Trail (paved)
Railroad / Tram
Ferry

Canoe Trail
Intracoastal Waterway
Wilderness Area
National Marine Sanctuary

Ranger Station/ Visitor Center/ Park Headquarters
Picnic Area
Pass

Point of Interest
Overlook / Viewpoint
Falls

Campground
Elevation
Dam

Swamp

ABBREVIATIONS

Cr.	Creek
Fk.	Fork
Hdqrs.	Headquarters
I.	Island
Mt.	Mount-ain
NAT. MON.	National Monument
N.F.	National Forest
N.S.T.	National Scenic Trail
N.W.R.	National Wildlife Refuge
Pk.	Peak
Rd.	Road
WILD.	Wilderness

Index

Boldface indicates illustrations.

Our National Parks

By John M. Thompson
Photographs by Phil Schermeister

Published by the National Geographic Society

John M. Fahey, Jr., President and Chief Executive Officer

Gilbert M. Grosvenor, Chairman of the Board

Nina D. Hoffman, Executive Vice President

Prepared by the Book Division

Kevin Mulroy, Senior Vice President and Publisher

Kristin Hanneman, Illustrations Director

Marianne R. Koszorus, Design Director

Barbara Brownell Grogan, Executive Editor

Staff for this Book

Rebecca Lescaze, Editor

Peggy Archambault, Art Director

Jane Menyawi, Illustrations Editor

Mary Jo Slazak, Researcher

Carl Mehler, Director of Maps

Thomas L. Gray, Map Researcher

Gregory Ugiansky, Map Production

R. Gary Colbert, Production Director

Lewis Bassford, Production Project Manager

Meredith C. Wilcox, Illustrations Specialist

Cameron Zotter, Production and Design Assistant

Robert Swanson, Indexer

Manufacturing and Quality Control

Christopher A. Liedel, Chief Financial Officer

Phillip L. Schlosser, Managing Director

John T. Dunn, Technical Director

Chris Brown, Manager

Founded in 1888, the National Geographic Society is one of the world's largest nonprofit scientific and educational organizations. Its mission is to increase and diffuse geographic knowledge while promoting conservation of the world's cultural and natural resources. National Geographic reflects the world through its five magazines, television programs, films, radio, books, videos, maps, interactive media and merchandise. National Geographic magazine, the Society's official journal, published in English and 27 local-language editions, is read by 40 million people each month in every country in the world. The National Geographic Channel reaches more than 260 million households in 27 languages in 160 countries. Nationalgeographic.com averages around 60 million page views per month. National Geographic has funded more than 8,000 scientific research projects and supports an education program combating geography illiteracy.

For more information,
log on to nationalgeographic.com;
AOL Keyword: NatGeo.

NATIONAL GEOGRAPHIC SOCIETY
1145 17th Street N.W.
Washington, D.C. 20036-4688 U.S.A.
Visit the Society's Web site at
www.nationalgeographic.com.

Library of Congress Cataloging-in-Publication Data

Thompson, John M. (Milliken), 1959–
   Our national parks : tours with rangers / by John M.
   Thompson ; photographs by Phil Schermeister
      p. cm
   ISBN 0-7922-5549-6 (Regular)
   ISBN 0-7922-5550-X (Deluxe)
   1. National parks and reserves—United States—
Guidebooks. 2. National parks and reserves—United
States—Pictorial works. 3. Park rangers—United
States—Interviews. I. Schermeister, Phil, ill. II. Title

E160.T49 2006
917.304'931—dc22

                        2005057689